PURELY & SIMPLY EVIL
BEHIND THE SCENES OF THE HALLOWEEN MOVIES

PURELY & SIMPLY EVIL

Halloween - 6
Halloween II - 28
Halloween III - 52
Halloween 4 - 70
Halloween 5 - 86
Halloween 6 - 100
Halloween H2O - 116
Halloween Resurrection - 132
Rob Zombie's Halloween - 146
Halloween II - 160

HALLOWEEN

The Night He Came Home.

Directed by John Carpenter

Written by John Carpenter and Debra Hill

Donald Pleasance (Dr. Sam Loomis)
Jamie Lee Curtis (Laurie Strode)
PJ Soles (Lynda van der Klok)
Nancy Loomis (Annie Brackett)
Charles Cyphers (Sheriff Leigh Brackett)
John Michael Graham (Bob Simms)
Nancy Stephens (Nurse Marian Chambers)
Brian Andrews (Tommy Doyle)
Kyle Richards (Lindsey Wallace)
Will Sandin (Young Michael Myers)
Nick Castle (The Shape)

HALLOWEEN

When first pitched by Irwin Yablans, the project was going to be called *The Babysitter Murders*. This actually stuck as the working title for a time until Yablans suggested theming the film to a certain October holiday.

Debra Hill would later produce the 1987 comedy *Adventures in Babysitting* during which two characters can be overheard watching *Halloween* on television. On a slightly related note, *Halloween 4*'s Danielle Harris later starred in the 1991 comedy *Don't Tell Mom the Babysitter's Dead*.

The film was originally going to be set across several days leading up to Halloween, but budgetary restraints necessitated compressing the storyline, thus reducing the need for additional locations and costume changes.

John Carpenter and Debra Hill split writing duties on the project. Hill was chiefly responsible for creating realistic dialogue between the female leads while Carpenter handled most of the Loomis/Michael conflict.

The script was reportedly written across three weeks.

John Carpenter was inspired to write his famous "blackest eyes" speech for Dr. Loomis after meeting a particularly chilling young psychiatric patient while on a college field trip to an asylum hospital in Kentucky.

John Carpenter named Michael Myers after the president of British film distributor Miracle Films, who had purchased the theatrical rights to distribute *Assault on Precinct 13*.

Laurie Strode was named after an early girlfriend of John Carpenter, which makes it all the more surprising that she actually survives the film.

Off screen character Ben Tramer was named after Bennett Tramer, a friend and peer of John Carpenter's at USC. The real-life Tramer would go on to write and produce more than seventy episodes of *Saved By the Bell* throughout its various incarnations.

Tributes to Alfred Hitchcock and *Psycho* abound: Dr. Sam Loomis is named after Marion Crane's boyfriend in *Psycho*. Marion Chambers' last name is named after Sheriff Chambers from the same film. Sheriff Leigh Brackett in *Halloween* is named after the framed screenwriter who twice wrote for Alfred Hitchcock's television series.

HALLOWEEN

Michael's name is only said twice in the film and never as a full name (as in "Michael Myers.") His full name is also never mentioned in the script, instead referring to him as "The Shape."

There has been much speculation over the years as to whether or not Michael's middle name is Audrey or Aubrey. The film's official novelization gives Audrey but the television cut appears to say Aubrey. *Halloween 4* would later complicate the matter further.

Michael was originally written to have a "dank, white face with blond hair" when unmasked. Obviously, this detail was changed during production.

Total Body Count: 7 (though two are dogs)

Dennis Quaid, who was then dating PJ Soles and nowhere near as popular as he is today, was wanted for the part of Bob. He was unable to take the role due to scheduling. John Michael Graham was cast instead.

Prior to appearing as Bob in *Halloween*, John Michael Graham had only done a handful of television commercials. He also appeared in *Grease* as an extra.

Both Peter Cushing and Christopher Lee declined the role of Dr. Loomis before it was offered to Donald Pleasance. Lee would later express regret over having not taken up the role. (In addition to being Hammer regulars, Cushing and Lee would both portray baddies in the *Star Wars* saga.)

Nick Castle never auditioned for the role of Michael Myers. He had no acting ambitions and had only wanted to make movies from behind the camera. He only planned to visit the set to observe filming. It was at the insistence of friend and colleague John Carpenter that he took on the role.

John Carpenter originally wanted Anne Lockhart, daughter of *Lassie's* June Lockhart, for the role of Laurie Strode.

Nine-year-old Kyle Richards was cast as young Lindsay Wallace. Richards had previously appeared in Tobe Hooper's *Eaten Alive* and in *Escape to Witch Mountain* alongside Donald Pleasance. Her aunt, Kim, appeared as Kathy in *Assault on Precinct 13*.

HALLOWEEN

If the young lady that played Judith Myers seemed unusually bodacious for a random American teenager, it is because actress Sandy Johnson was actually a Playboy Playmate for the June 1974 issue.

Halloween had its share of onset romances. John Carpenter and Debra Hill were a couple and Nancy Loomis was then married to Tommy Lee Wallace.

Donald Pleasance was admittedly less than enamored with the script, but took the role anyway because his daughter, Angela, was a fan of *Assault on Precinct 13*.

John Carpenter reported casting PJ Soles after seeing her performance in *Rock 'n' Roll High School*.

Tony Moran is the brother of *Happy Days'* Erin Moran.

Nick Castle would later joke about being replaced as the face of Michael Myers at New Jerey's Monster Mania 17: "I guess they didn't want someone as handsome as me."

Veteran actor Donald Pleasance earned $20,000 for his work on the film. Newcomer Jamie Lee Curtis earned $8,000. Fledgling actor Tony Moran was paid $250 for his one day of work. Non-actor Nick Castle earned $25 per day as the Shape.

John Carpenter's two demands, both outrageous for a novice filmmaker, was to have his name above the title and the power of final cut.

John Carpenter took a $10,000 fee for directing as well a back-end profit sharing deal.

Of the three leading ladies, only Jamie Lee Curtis was a teenager at the time of filming. PJ Soles was twenty-six and Nancy Loomis was twenty-eight.

Jamie Lee Curtis was only able to appear in the film because she was on hiatus from *Operation Petticoat*, which was between its first and second seasons. The show was based on the 1959 film of the same name, which starred Curtis' father, Tony. When *Operation Petticoat* returned for its second season, it did so in bizarre fashion without almost any of the cast from season one. Curtis was among the dumped leads. The show was cancelled ten episodes later.

HALLOWEEN

Although it was not entirely responsible for her winning the role, the fact that Jamie Lee Curtis' mother, Janet Leigh, was the iconic shower victim in *Psycho* certainly did not hurt her chances at landing the Laurie Strode role.

The budget was so choked that most of the cast had to wear their own clothes. Jamie Lee Curtis reportedly made a trip to JC Penny's to pick out her character's wardrobe, which totaled under $100.

John Carpenter cast himself as the voice of Annie's boyfriend, Paul.

The film is set in the fictional town of Haddonfield, Illinois, which is named for Debra Hill's hometown of Haddonfield, New Jersey.

Smith's Grove Warren County Sanitarium was named for Smith's Grove, Kentucky, a town not far from Bowling Green where John Carpenter grew up.

Mountains can be seen behind Dr. Loomis in the highway-side telephone booth. This is not possible in Illinois.

At the time, the Myers House was unoccupied and owned by a church. It was in real life every bit as ugly and decrepit as it appeared on film, except for the one night late in filming when the production team were required to spruce it up and furnish the inside in order to capture the opening scene. Being that *Halloween* lensed out of season, bags of painted leaves had to be spread across exterior locations and then rebagged for use in other scenes. Gourds were imported and painted to look like pumpkins.

The opening credits were initially scripted to feature the Shape's mask against darkness rather than the pumpkin eventually seen in the finished film.

The point-of-view shot that begins the movie was not originally scripted to begin in front of the Myers house but instead *behind* it. John Carpenter also considered opening the film down the street from the Myers homestead and having Michael discover a mask to wear while en route home.

The opening scene appears to be one uninterrupted shot. While an impressive feat of cinematography, it does contain three subtle cuts.

HALLOWEEN

John Carpenter was inspired to attempt the long-take opening shot after seeing a similar sequence in Orson Welle's *Touch of Evil*.

PJ Soles's Lynda says "Totally" eleven times in the film.

Although filming occurred across twenty days, Donald Pleasance's role was wrapped in only five.

Brian Andrews's role as Tommy Doyle was wrapped in four days near the end of production.

The dead Phelps Towing mechanic is played by an uncredited Barry Bernardi, who would later produce the next two *Halloween* sequels.

Will Sandin was unavailable to film the point-of-view shot that began the film. Sandin's hands were doubled by Debra Hill, making her the first performer to play Michael in the entire series. Look closely and you can spot her recently manicured fingers reaching for the kitchen knife just before the murder. This is much easier seen on Blu-Ray.

Halloween was not the first film to utilize a Steadicam rig, but it was among the first several productions. Cinematographer Dean Cundey was an enormous advocate of the technique.

Will Sandin's preparation prior to filming his one shot as young Michael Myers went entirely to waste. The actor reported practicing trying to look as scary as he possibly could, but was instead instructed by John Carpenter once on set to simply look blank.

At 5'10, Nick Castle stood as the second shortest shape behind Dick Warlock. He was also the second oldest - again behind Warlock.

Blue Oyster Cult's *Don't Fear the Reaper* plays while Annie and Laurie drive not only because it is an ass-kicking song to include in a horror movie, but because it also subtly refers to who is following behind them (the Shape).

The scene inside between Laurie and Annie inside the latter's car was improvised by the performers and directed by Debra Hill in order to extend the film's short runtime.

Tommy's Halloween costume is an Alphan uniform from *Space: 1999*.

HALLOWEEN

The masterful shot of Laurie backing into a doorframe and the Shape slowly appearing from darkness was achieved by having cinematographer Dean Cundey place a dimmer light on Nick Castle's masked face and very slowly dialing up the amount of light.

The movie playing on television Halloween night is 1951's *The Thing from Another World*, which John Carpenter would later remake as *The Thing*.

Donald Pleasance much preferred John Carpenter's mostly bloodless approach as opposed to the slasher craze that followed – including *Halloween*'s own sequels.

Because the movie was filmed wildly out of order (as most movies are), John Carpenter invented a "Fear Meter" he would use to help Jamie Lee Curtis with her performance. The director would give his actress a number from one to ten – depending on the scene – that would inform her of how terrified Laurie would be, ten being the most terrified.

Lynda's "See anything you like?" line was not in the shooting script but rather improvised on set by PJ Soles.

It has been joked about that Tommy Lee Wallace, being responsible for most of the props and sets, would double Nick Castle anytime Michael had to break or burst through something (the kitchen door and closet door scenes being examples of this). This was because the filmmakers could not afford for multiple takes or multiple breakable props.

The iconic head-tilt following Bob's murder was not scripted, but improvised on set by Nick Castle.

Nick Castle is said to have kept the mood onset light with his own brand of humor. Production photos show him clowning around in the mask, kissing Jamie Lee Curtis and drinking Dr. Pepper through it. One outtake captured following the climactic shot of the Shape lying motionless on the ground reveals a masked Castle dancing himself off camera for the subsequent shot where Dr. Loomis looks down to an empty yard.

Stuntman Jim Winburn doubled Nick Castle for the fall off the balcony at the end of the film.

The production's dark lighting scheme was only partway intentional. The crew simply did not have enough equipment to light entire sets.

HALLOWEEN

Donald Pleasance theorized that the last scene where. Dr. Loomis sees Michael gone could be played two different ways, either "He's gone!" or "I knew this would happen." John Carpenter had the actor perform it both ways after which he sided with the actor's preference, which was "I knew this would happen."

Although it is perhaps the most oft-told anecdote from the series, I would be remiss not to mention the origin of Michael Myers' mask. The shooting script was somewhat imprecise in its description of said prop. So Tommy Lee Wallace prepared two potential masks for John Carpenter to consider, both from Don Post. The first was a generic-looking Emmett Kelly clown mask and the second, a $1.98 Captain Kirk mask that had been painted white, given widened eyeholes and stripped of its sideburns. The Kirk mask won out, becoming the iconic face of the Shape we all know so well. At least two masks were made for filming, though some reports put the number at three.

The prop knife used most often during filming was not made of rubber or wood, but an actual kitchen knife heavily dulled by a crewmember to prevent injury.

It was originally hoped that famed mask maker Don Post would create the masks seen in the film. The producers knew this would be a costly process, one that they could not afford, but contacted Post anyway hoping to secure his services by offering him a percentage of the project's back-end profits. No stranger to these "no money down" offers from movie productions, Post declined.

The poster on Laurie's wall is of a painting by Belgian artist James Ensor who was known to paint his subjects wearing grotesque masks.

Michael's ride was a 1976 Ford LTD station wagon, which was rented for the production by Tommy Lee Wallace.

Although the Shape can be seen breaking the passenger window to Marion Chambers's station wagon during his escape, it is magically repaired in subsequent scenes such as while stalking Tommy Doyle as he leaves school.

The Black Fleetwood that sits in the Strode's driveway belonged to John Carpenter.

When not appearing onscreen, the Phelps Garage truck was used to cater box lunches to the cast and crew.

HALLOWEEN

The opening credits pumpkin was carved by Tommy Lee Wallace associate Randy Moore, who also handled the lettering on Judith's tombstone. Moore would go on to consult with Wallace on *Halloween III* and serve as Art Director on Wallace's *Fright Night Part 2*, the *Fright Night* remake and *The Avengers*.

Although difficult to see in the final film, Tony Moran was outfitted with a bloodless eye wound from the coat hanger injury that Laurie gave his character. It stood as one of the film's few makeup effects.

Reportedly, Tommy Lee Wallace created at least three masks for the film, though unconfirmed reports put the number as being as high as five.

Tommy's oddly-named comic books were all fictional titles invented just for the movie. The comics he is actually holding, however, are mostly issues of *Howard the Duck*.

The film's score was composed and performed by John Carpenter but credited to the Bowling Green Philharmonic

Orchestra. In reality, no such group exists. The faux-band name was a reference to Carpenter's hometown of Bowling Green, Kentucky.

Artist Bob Gleason painted the film's iconic poster artwork.

Gleason, either intentionally or unintentionally, painted a hidden face into the knuckles of the poster art, known to fans as "The Face in the Hand."

The film premiered at the AMC Empire Theater on October 25, 1978 in Kansas City, Missouri.

Oblivious to just how good *Halloween* would actually be, Tony Moran actually threw out his invitation to its premiere screening. He later saw it in an ordinary theater and was pleasantly surprised.

Will Sandin attended the premiere screening with his family and was forced to leave partway through when his little sister became too scared of what was happening onscreen.

Despite sporting one of the horror genre's most memorable soundtracks, *Halloween* score was not formally released on record until 1983 – five years after the film's release.

HALLOWEEN

More than thirty years after *Halloween*, writer Greg Mitchell released *White Ghost* through the official *Halloween Comics* website. The short story revealed what happened in the encounter between the Phelps Garage mechanic and the Shape.

Halloween grossed $47 million domestically, far and above making it the most successful independent film of its time.

The film's novelization was released in 1979 and re-printed in 1982 and 1983. It has long been out of print and is considered a collector's item.

The film's novelization includes a bizarrtee subplot about Michael's grandfather having gone similarly mad in the late 1890s. The story is told as hearsay from Sheriff Brackett to Dr. Loomis, who is surprised to learn something new that has not previously been in Michael's Smith's Grove case file.

Anchor Bay Entertainment has released *Halloween* onto DVD across approximately 8,462 special editions. (Okay, so the number is closer to seven. *But it is still a lot!*)

Nick Castle was allowed to keep one of the masks after filming since there was zero expectation of a sequel at that time. He reported placing it on a foam head and hanging it on his wall for several years as one would a stuffed hunting trophy.

Although the coveted television rights to *Halloween* were sold to NBC in 1980 for $4 million, it would not air on the network until the following year just before the titular holiday.

Halloween was very tightly scripted and consequently had no actual deleted scenes. John Carpenter did utilize the *Halloween II* crew in 1981 to film three new scenes for the first film in order to pad its NBC debut into a fuller runtime.

Kyle Richards would go on to become one of the first *Real Housewives of Beverly Hills* and, in a twist far more horrifying than anything in the *Halloween* franchise, she would become an aunt to Paris Hilton.

The film was later adapted into an Atari game in 1983, which turned out to be far bloodier than anything seen in the film itself (Michael cuts off Laurie's head).

HALLOWEEN

Robert Englund's Doc Halloran in *Behind the Mask: The Rise of Leslie Vernon* was a tribute to Donald Pleasance's role and performance from this film.

Halloween was parodied in 1982's *Wacko*, which starred Joe Don Baker, George Kennedy, Andrew Dice Clay, Elizabeth Daily and Charles Napier. It was directed by B-movie legend and *MST3k* favorite Greydon Clark.

Several years after *Halloween*'s release, Don Post Studios attempted to negotiate a deal to produce officially licensed Michael Myers masks. Much to their disappointment, they were turned down by the rights holders and instead released "The Mask," which although quite popular was arguably one of the worst Michael Myers masks, authorized or unauthorized, ever to hit the market.

After *Halloween*, Jamie Lee Curtis hosted *Coming Soon* and Donald Pleasance hosted *Terror in the Aisles*, both clip-documentaries on the horror genre. The latter was included as a supplemental feature on Universal's initial Blu-Ray offering of *Halloween II*.

In a 2001 episode of *Who Wants to be a Millionaire?*, one question asked upon what other famous mask was the original Michael Myers mask based. The contestant answered the question correctly to win $500,000, nearly twice the budget of *Halloween*.

In early 2009, super fan and rising filmmaker Kenny Caperton custom built an impressive replica of the Myers House in Hillsborough, North Carolina. He has since opened its doors to fans for Halloween celebrations and special events. Learn more at: http://myershousenc.com.

Halloween spawned a sequel in 1981. If this is news to you, turn the page and let me blow your mind!

BEHIND THE SCENES OF THE HALLOWEEN MOVIES

HALLOWEEN

HALLOWEEN II

More of the Night He Came Home.

Directed by Rick Rosenthal

Written by John Carpenter and Debra Hill

Donald Pleasance (Dr. Sam Loomis)
Jamie Lee Curtis (Laurie Strode)
Charles Cyphers (Sheriff Leigh Brackett)
Lance Guest (Jimmy)
Gloria Gifford (Mrs. Alves)
Leo Rossi (Budd)
Pamela Susan Shoop (Karen)
Tawny Moyers (Jill)
Hunter von Leer (Deputy Gary Hunt)
Dick Warlock (The Shape)

HALLOWEEN II

Dino De Laurentiis bought the rights to make the sequel for $2 million with distribution and ownership through Universal Pictures. He opted to retain the creative team behind the original – John Carpenter and Debra Hill.

Although John Carpenter and Debra Hill returned to write and produce, Carpenter had no interest in actually directing the film. He did, however, agree to help compose music for the production.

John Carpenter later reported resentfully approaching *Halloween II* with a six-pack of beer every night he tried to write the screenplay, feeling that there was no more story left to tell. It was out of sheer desperation that he concocted the brother/sister twist between Michael and Laurie.

As a result of the De Laurentiis buyout, Irwin Yablans and Moustapha Akkad were Executive Producers in name only and had nothing to do with the film.

Tommy Lee Wallace was offered the opportunity to direct, but declined. He has since confessed his hatred for the script and direction in which the film was taken.

This film marks the directorial debut of Rick Rosenthal, who was hand chosen by John Carpenter based on a short film he made called Toyer.

Halloween II was originally going to unfold several years after the first film and be set inside of a high-rise apartment building where Laurie Strode now lived.

There was serious discussion early on that *Halloween II* might be filmed in 3-D. That practically the entire film was set at night ultimately convinced the filmmakers not to undertake this approach, night scenes being especially difficult to film using the 3-D processes of the time.

One unintended retroactive effect of the new brother/sister twist is that it makes Laurie Strode's father come off as a sadistic asshole. It means that he sent his adopted daughter to drop off a key at the house where her brother murdered their sister on the anniversary of the killing. It is creepy if you think about it long enough.

This is the most time compressed *Halloween* film in the entire franchise, unfolding across roughly ten to twelve hours.

HALLOWEEN II

Although not filmed, the shooting script contained an additional death scene: the female WWAR news producer was to have encountered a flat tire while en route to Haddonfield Memorial Hospital. Michael was to have been hiding in her trunk and killed her upon pulling over. This would have explained how Michael traveled to the hospital so quickly.

WWAR Reporter Robert Mundy and his news crew were originally scripted to show up at Haddonfield Memorial Hospital only to be turned away by Mrs. Alves. This scene still appears in the film's novelization.

While *Halloween II* outrightly mentions the festival of Samhain, it is not the first entry in the series to do so. Samhain was also mentioned in the novelization of the original *Halloween*.

According to the script, the ages of the hospital staff are as follows: Janet is nineteen, Jimmy is twenty-one, Budd is twenty-four and Karen is also twenty-four.

Mrs. Alves' full name was Virginia D. Alves.

The script featured a line omitted from the film that established Bud as a Vietnam veteran who criticizes Jimmy as being a "college boy" that wouldn't have survived fifteen minutes in the war.

The *Halloween II* script continues referring to Michael in its descriptive action as "The Shape." The end credits continue this tradition as well.

Whereas no character in the original *Halloween* ever actually said Michael's full name aloud, it is spoken in this film eleven times.

Universal Pictures gave *Halloween II* a budget of $2.5 million, more than eight times the budget of the original film.

Total Body Count: 10 (though Ben Tramer's death was not at the hands of the Shape)

Tony Moran was invited back to play Michael Myers, but uninterested in reprising the role. He did grant permission for the sequel to use his performance from the first film, however.

HALLOWEEN II

Nick Castle was not asked to reprise his role as the Shape because the producers knew he was busy with his directorial debut feature, *TAG: The Assassination Game*, but also because they knew Castle had no interest in an acting career. (For anyone curious, *TAG* is a forgotten film that starred Robert Carradine, Bruce Abbott and Linda Hamilton in her first role.)

Dick Warlock was originally only hired as stunt coordinator for the film. The story goes that he spotted Michael's mask sitting on a desk while walking through the production offices. He put it on and began stalking the hallways, eventually stopping in silence at Rick Rosenthal's door. Rosenthal liked his performance and suggested him to Debra Hill, who gave her approval.

At 5'9, Dick Warlock is the shortest performer to play Michael Myers in the entire franchise. He was given added stature through the use of shoe lifts.

Dick Warlock has since confessed that he had not seen the original *Halloween* prior to being cast as Michael Myers. He did view it several times after being cast in the role, however, and found two memorable scenes upon which he based his performance. They were Nick Castle's head tilt after murdering Bob and Tommy Lee Wallace's slow sit-up after the closet scene.

Dick Warlock would be the first stuntman cast in the role of Michael Myers, a trend that would last until 2007 with Rob Zombie's remake.

Five performers in total returned from the original *Halloween* for this film: Jamie Lee Curtis, Donald Pleasance, Nancy Loomis, Charles Cyphers and Nancy Stephens.

This film marks the sixth and final appearance of Charles Cyphers in a John Carpenter production.

Having both aged considerably and left the profession, Will Sandin was unavailable to reprise his role as Young Michael Myers for the sequel's flashback sequences. Adam Gunn takes over the role in this film.

Rick Rosenthal handpicked several cast members from acting classes being taught at The Beverly Hills Playhouse, which he frequented. These performers included Ana Alicia, Leo Rossi and Gloria Gifford.

HALLOWEEN II

Mrs. Alves was originally written as a fifty-year-old Caucasian nurse, but the role was changed to a younger African-American part to accommodate Gloria Gifford. Though the age and race of the character changed, the sternness and demise did not.

Jamie Lee Curtis receives top billing on this film, despite only having roughly twenty-six minutes of screen time as a mostly bed-ridden Laurie Strode.

Not counting the flashback from the original film, Jamie Lee Curtis speaks roughly eighty words across the entire film, four of which are "help."

This is the only *Halloween* film that Donald Pleasance appears in for which he does not receive top billing.

Donald Pleasance later told Fangoria in issue 89 that he attended several story meetings about his character prior to filming *Halloween II*. It was during these meetings that he made several "real insane" suggestions, all of which John Carpenter rightly ignored.

Nancy Loomis makes a brief cameo as Annie's corpse (though watch closely and you can see her eyes flutter in a very un-corpse-like manner.)

Funnyman Dana Carvey makes his big screen debut here in a non-speaking role as the TV station assistant wearing the blue trucker hat. You can see him early in the film at the Myers House and also at the film's end walking behind Laurie as she's wheeled into the ambulance.

Both Jeffrey Kramer and Lance Guest would go on to appear in the Jaws franchise as Deputy Hendricks in *Jaws/Jaws 2* and Michael Brody in *Jaws: The Revenge*, respectively.

Hunter Von Leer had not seen the original *Halloween* prior to being cast and elected not to watch it even after being cast, instead opting to focus solely on his character.

Several other cast members such as Pamela Susan Shoop and Gloria Gifford had also not seen the first film. Debra Hill arranged a screening for those interested in seeing it.

Barry Bernardi serves as associate producer on this film after his uncredited appearance as the murdered Phelps Towing mechanic in the original film.

HALLOWEEN II

The intersection where Dr. Loomis encounters Ben Tramer is the same intersection where Tommy Doyle runs up to Laurie Strode en route to school in the first film.

Halloween II returned to use the same Pasadena Myers House as the original film, then located on Meridian Avenue. It would be the last film in the series to feature this particular location before the structure was moved to Mission Street to avoid demolition in 1987.

While the address of the Myers House is mentioned as being 45 Lampkin Lane, the house's front exterior clearly sports the numbers 709 (as in 709 Meridian Avenue, its original location) and not 45.

At one point, a character refers to the murders happening in Orange Grove. Both the Doyle and Wallace houses from the original Halloween were located on Orange Grove Avenue in West Hollywood.

For those curious, Haddonfield Memorial Hospital was written to have three floors: Main Floor, Radiology Floor and Maintenance Basement.

Principal photography began on April 18, 1981.

Jamie Lee Curtis had trimmed her long locks short since the original Halloween and had to wear a wig for the entirety of her performance in *Halloween II*.

In the original *Halloween*, Dr. Loomis fires six shots at Michael. In the opening of *Halloween II*, he fires seven shots but later maintains he only fired six.

Overall, Michael is shot by Dr. Loomis' revolver thirteen times throughout this film (six off the balcony, five in the hospital lobby and twice by Laurie).

Dick Warlock recreates Jim Winburn's balcony stunt from the original *Halloween* for this film's opening. The angle used makes it fairly obvious the stuntman backs onto a ramp.

Dick Warlock cameos unmasked as a patrolman moments after the Ben Tramer incident.

Both of Dick Warlock's sons also cameo in the film. Lance Warlock appears in a cowboy hat carrying a boom box in downtown Haddonfield. Billy Warlock appears as Craig, one of the teenagers concerned about Ben Tramer.

HALLOWEEN II

It was originally written for the boom box carried by Lance Warlock's character to be playing Mr. Sandman as well.

While John Carpenter's influence was felt throughout the production, he only visited the set twice. Debra Hill, however, maintained a constant presence on set.

In addition to making a cameo as the corpse of Annie Brackett, Nancy Loomis also provides the telephone voice of Alice's friend moments before her untimely murder.

The romance continued on *Halloween II* where Rick Rosenthal met his future wife, Nancy Stephens.

The water in the hot tub scene was reportedly none too clean, which led to Pamela Susan Shoop getting an ear infection from being dunked so many times. Although the water appears scalding hot onscreen, it was actually very cold.

Although the script cites the hot tub's temperature as peaking a 127 degrees Fahrenheit, the gauge goes much higher than this in the actual movie.

Michael was originally to throw Karen's entire body into the hot tub rather than simply tossing her onto the floor.

That Karen's death scene is foreshadowed long before it happens is lost on most viewers. She can first be heard lamenting that the Halloween party she left featured bobbing for apples. She dies by drowning in a tub full of water. (How about them apples? God, awful pun. Apologies.)

Bud was originally going to be seen post-strangulation prior to Karen's kill with a stethoscope jammed into his mouth.

Pamela Susan Shoop's nude scene, which she found more difficult to perform than initially thought, was filmed across two days. The actress has since shared that she cried while driving to set the second day. In an attempt to make her more comfortable, Rick Rosenthal requested the male crew strip down to their underwear, which they immediately refused to do. This only re-enforced for Shoop how difficult the scene was.

Rick Rosenthal worked closely with returning cinematographer Dean Cundey to recreate John Carpenter's visual style on the sequel. This included again using subjective angles to communicate the Shape's point-of-view.

HALLOWEEN II

The film playing on television is *Night of the Living Dead*, which was likely chosen for its public domain status. The audio as heard inside the Elrod house does not match up with audio from the actual film, however. In the film, the line "They're coming to get you, Barbara" is not immediately followed by music, though the sudden music cue when Mrs. Elrod discovers the blood makes for a nice moment.

Although the script mentions Michael only having one visible eye due to his coat-hanger injury in the first film, the makeup department appears to have ignored this detail.

Ana Alicia sustained an eye injury requiring stitches when a stunt for her character's death scene went awry. After Janet receives the hypodermic needle to the temple from the Shape, it was written that she would collapse backward. The set, however, had not been properly prepared for the take and Alicia fell face first into the edge of a desk, sustaining the injury and requiring her subsequent scenes to be shot at an angle that did not reveal her entire face.

Halloween II is the only sequel in the franchise to actually reach daylight on November 1st.

Dick Warlock was required to perform the ending's dangerous fire-walk stunt twice on account of the filmmakers being unsatisfied with the first take. His son assisted him as part of the team that prepped him for the stunt.

Although Deputy Hunt hands Dr. Loomis a smoke and a lighter, the cigarette never touches the doctor's lips and he never returns the lighter. It is this same lighter than Dr. Loomis uses to blow up the hospital at the film's climax. In the script, it was Dr. Loomis that produced the cigarettes from his coat pocket. The script continues with Loomis trying to return Hunt's lighter, but is told instead, "Keep it."

That Bud sang a perverse version of Amazing Grace owed to the fact that the song was in the public domain and cost nothing to license. John Carpenter and Debra Hill had originally scripted for him to sing a perverse version of Unchained Melody.

Donald Pleasance performed his own stunt for the scene where Dr. Loomis is stabbed by Michael and falls to the ground.

Dick Warlock has jokingly referred to the film's conclusion at personal appearances as the "Flick your Bic" ending.

HALLOWEEN II

One oft-told anecdote from the set involved Tawny Moyer being hoisted up by Michael's stab using the same harness that allowed Julie Andrews to fly in *Mary Poppins*. A strategically placed piece of balsa wood allowed Dick Warlock to convincingly stab into the actresses back.

Principal photography wrapped on May 25, 1981.

Jamie Shourt, who created the film's memorable opening title sequence, also created special effects for *The Blues Brothers*, *Airplane!* and the original *Star Wars*.

It has been widely reported and confirmed that, despite appearing different, the mask in *Halloween II* was the same mask used in the original. Two different stories exist for where exactly it had been since the first film. Debra Hill claims to have kept the mask crumpled in a box under her bed for several years, thus altering its appearance. Nick Castle, however, claims that he took ownership of an original *Halloween* mask after that film wrapped. The filmmaker reported that Hill eventually called wanting to borrow the mask for a sequel and that he never received it back.

The dangerous "swishing" scalpel that Michael chases after Laurie with was, in actuality, an eraser on a stick for non-close-ups.

The famous "Blood Tears" scene was only shot once. Blood tubes lined the interior of Dick Warlock's mask and he triggered the effect with a handheld bulb.

John Carpenter did not find Rick Rosenthal's original cut of the film scary whatsoever, famously likening it to an episode of the hospital-drama *Quincy*. He opted to write and direct three days of additional scenes to amp up the film's gore and violence content in the aftermath of slasher films such as *Friday the 13th*.

Among the scenes added by John Carpenter after filming was the introduction and immediate kill of Alice. This late addition is further evidenced by the scene not appearing in the original shooting script.

That the film was bookended with Mr. Sandman by the Chordettes was not based on a random whim. John Carpenter and Debra Hill actually included the song in their screenplay.

HALLOWEEN II

The film marks the first appearance of Composer Alan Howarth on the soundtrack. Having just finished work on *Escape from New York*, he would co-score *Halloween II* with John Carpenter. Howarth would go on to score the next four Halloween sequels.

As in the original film, Tony Moran's Michael is mistakenly listed in the end credits as being twenty-three-years-old when he is actually only twenty-one.

The film's sole "Special Thanks" credit goes to Gene and Louise Bramson, who owned one of the houses used in *Halloween* and the beginning of *Halloween II*.

Halloween II was famously re-edited for broadcast on television, resulting in numerous alternate and deleted scenes. This version, known as "the TV Cut," contains more than five-dozen changes from the theatrical version of the film.

In a line cut from the ending, Dr. Loomis was to have shouted at Michael: "Die, damn you, die!"

The most notable deleted scene from the film is the extended ending. As Laurie rides away in the ambulance, a sheet-covered figure rises behind her. Startled, she spins around to see it is only Jimmy who is also being transferred to another hospital due to his head injury. Laurie cries and says, "We made it!"

Although performers for young Laurie Strode and both her parents appear in the film's ending credits, they do not actually appear in the theatrical film itself.

Jamie Lee Curtis hosted *Saturday Night Live* four months before filming began on December 13, 1980. In her opening monologue, she told the audience she understood that people had set expectations of certain performers. For example, Steve Martin would always have to say "I'm a wild and crazy guy" and Rodney Dangerfeild would have to say "I get no respect!" She then told the audience she knew what they all wanted from her since she had appeared in *The Fog* and *Halloween*... before unleashing her finest scream.

Somewhat strangely, *Halloween II* figures into the plot of issue 217 of *The Amazing Spider-Man* comic, which was written while the movie was still being filmed. In the issue, Spidey actually lets Hydroman escape so that he can see

HALLOWEEN II

this movie. After purchasing a ticket, Peter Parker asks a friend leaving the theater how the movie was. The friend responds, "It was the grandmother who planted the bomb," thus ruining the movie for Peter. (But not for the reader, fortunately!)

Donald Pleasance hosted *Saturday Night Live* the day after *Halloween II* opened in theaters. It was also one day after NBC held the world broadcast premiere of the original *Halloween*.

Halloween II opened on 1,211 theaters domestically.

The film debuted with a $7.4 million opening weekend.

Believing that the Michael Myers storyline had finally been put to rest and it was no longer needed, Dick Warlock was allowed to keep his mask and costume, which he later sold to a fan many years later.

The film was adapted into a novelization by Jack Martin, pen name for Denis Etchison.

Six months after the release of this film, another slasher-terrorizes-a-hospital picture was released into theaters called *Visiting Hours*. Starring Lee Grant, Michael Ironside and William Shatner, it appears to owe more than a little to *Halloween II*. Although it wrapped filming days before Michael Myer's return hit theaters, its skull-centric poster and similar sounding music greatly evoke *Halloween II*.

In 1982, thirty-four-year-old Richard Delmer Boyer of El Monte, CA stabbed an elderly couple to death inside their Fullerton, CA home. He was reportedly under the influence of cocaine and PCP and, after having seen *Halloween II*, claimed that he believed he was under attack from Michael Myers. This defense did not hold up and he was convicted of the double-murder and subsequently sentenced to death.

Nick Castle saw the film on account of his friends, John Carpenter and Debra Hill, having made it and not because he is particularly fond of the genre or franchise. He cast Lance Guest in *The Last Starfighter* after seeing his performance as Jimmy.

Domestically speaking, *Halloween II* went on to become the 30th highest grossing film of 1981 with more than $25 million, besting *Escape from New York, Friday the 13th: Part*

HALLOWEEN II

II, The Final Confclit: Omen III, The Howling, Scanners and *My Bloody Valentine*. The only horror film to gross higher was *An American Werewolf in London*.

Jamie Lee Curtis does not look back fondly on this film, often citing her involvement as an obligation to John Carpenter and Debra Hill for the success they helped her achieve. She told Fangoria magazine while promoting the seventh film that it was a "mistake" to have made.

Donald Pleasance also later told Fangoria in their 89th issue that he was not as fond of *Halloween II* for being "too violent" and lacking "the intelligent quality" of the original film.

In 2011, Universal Studios released *Halloween II: The 30th Anniversary Edition* onto Blu-Ray. Despite being criminally light on extras (despite the presence of the fantastic *Terror in the Aisles* documentary), the release inexplicably replaced the "Moustapha Akkad Presents" title card in the film's opening credits with "Universal, an MCA Company, Presents." *Halloween* fans immediately began to complain as did the official *Halloween* website. Universal soon corrected the title card on all outgoing copies and offered replacement discs to those unhappy with the change.

Universal Studios didn't officially license a *Halloween II* Michael Myers mask until 2012, a staggering thirty-one years after the film's release.

BEHIND THE SCENES OF THE HALLOWEEN MOVIES

HALLOWEEN II

HALLOWEEN III

The Night No One Comes Home.

Directed by Tommy Lee Wallace

Written by Tommy Lee Wallace

Tom Atkins (Dr. Daniel Challis)
Stacey Nelkin (Ellie Grimbridge)
Dan O'Herlihy (Conal Cochran)
Garn Stephens (Marge)
Dick Warlock (Robot Henchman)
Jonathan Terry (Starker)

HALLOWEEN III

Universal Pictures met with John Carpenter and Debra Hill immediately following *Halloween II*'s successful opening weekend to discuss plans for a third film. It would be in theaters one year later.

Moustapha Akkad personally advised against a Shape-less *Halloween III*, but was outvoted.

Irwin Yablans was not consulted on the production at all, making him Executive Producer in name only. He too disagreed with steering the franchise away from Haddonfield. This film would mark the last time he featured as producer of any kind on a *Halloween* production.

The "witchcraft in the computer age" story angle originally owed to Debra Hill.

For a brief time during early development, John Carpenter had brought Joe Dante on board to direct the third *Halloween*. Movement on the project was slow, however, and Dante soon left the project to co-direct *The Twilight Zone* movie for Steven Spielberg, which was advancing at a much faster clip.

Despite only being on the project a short time, Joe Dante's contributions were enormously important. It was he who suggested the production hire Nigel Kneale to write the screenplay. Kneale was perhaps best known for creating the heroic scientist Professor Bernard Quatermass.

Nigel Kneale was admittedly not a fan of the first two *Halloween* films and thought Donald Pleasance was wasted in the role of Dr. Loomis. He was, however, interested in writing a *Halloween* story that was not slasher-centric.

It took Nigel Kneale six weeks to write his first draft of the screenplay.

While John Carpenter, Debra Hill and Tommy Lee Wallace all liked Nigel Kneale's screenplay very much, Dino De Laurentiis did not and recommended numerous changes including more violence and gore be injected into the movie. Kneale was immediately hostile to these requests and left the project, later suing to have his name removed from the credits.

After Nigel Kneale's exit, an uncredited John Carpenter rewrote the screenplay, which still did not satisfy Dino De Laurentiis. Tommy Lee Wallace followed Carpenter

HALLOWEEN III

in rewriting the script, finally gaining the approval of De Laurentiis. Wallace later estimated that 60% of the finished film owed to Nigel Kneale's original script with the remaining 40% coming from his and Carpenter's rewrites.

Despite walking away from *Halloween III*, Nigel Keane reported having a promising idea for *Halloween IV* that involved ghosts and would have continued the anthology direction of the series. He abandoned it, however, deeming it far too similar to *Poltergeist*.

Nigel Kneale later heaped criticism upon the addition of the Stonehenge sub-plot and opening skull-crushing scene.

Halloween III had a $2.5 million budge, same as its predecessor.

Debra Hill is credited with suggesting Tommy Lee Wallace direct the film. Wallace later revealed being surprised to receive such a call, having thought the bridge might have been burned when he turned down the same opportunity on *Halloween II*.

Not unlike Rick Rosenthal on *Halloween II*, this film marked Tommy Lee Wallace's directorial debut.

This film keyed into Tommy Lee Wallace's personal belief that the greatest villains in our world are not unstoppable slashers but rather corporate types. They wear not bloody coveralls but rather finely tailored suits.

Halloween III starts earlier than any other movie in the series by beginning on Saturday October 23.

Tommy Lee Wallace reportedly wanted Conal Cochran's robot army to be entirely redheaded, an idea that was neither feasible nor particularly good.

Famed mask maker Don Post created the three masks featured prominently throughout this film. He took very little for his services upfront in exchange for the exclusive merchandising rights to the film.

Conal Cochran's mention of Samhain while talking to Dr. Challis harkens back to Michael writing the same word on the blackboard in *Halloween II*.

Total Body Count: 23 (thirteen of which were robots)

HALLOWEEN III

The titular witch originally referred to Conal Cochran's character, who was to be a 3,000 year old demon.

In the original script, Dr. Challis was much more of a deadbeat character than in the eventual film. It was through Tommy Lee Wallace's rewrite and the eventual casting of Tom Atkins that he was made more likable.

The opening sequence in which a computer digitally creates a Halloween pumpkin heavily recalls the previous two film's opening sequences. It would be the last *Halloween* film to begin this way.

The shooting script originally saw the film open with the following poem: "Halloween will come, will come, witchcraft will be set agoing, demons will be at full speed running in every pass, avoid the road children, children."

Tommy Lee Wallace maintains in public appearances today that he had no idea exactly when Ellie became a robot.

Curiously, the town's curfew apparently does not apply to the liquor store from which Dr. Challis shops.

One of the most criticized goofs regarding the film involves the problem of the timing of the "Big Giveaway at 9." This would have to unfold across at least four different time zones in the United States alone. If unsynchronized, the West Coast would experience Conal Cochran's Halloween treat three hours after the East Coast.

Jamie Lee Curtis was originally offered a role in this film, but politely declined. She did still cameo, however, as the phone operator and as the voice announcing the town's curfew.

Former "Shape" Dick Warlock returned not only as stunt coordinator, but as one of Conal Cochran's robot henchman as well.

It was Debra Hill who originally suggested Tom Atkins for the film, having worked with him recently on both *The Fog* and *Escape from New York*.

This film marks the debut appearance of Joshua John Miller as Dr. Challis' son. Horror fans might be more familiar with his father, Jason Miller who portrayed Father Karras from *The Exorcist*.

HALLOWEEN III

Conal Cochran was the first Irish character that Irishman actor Dan O'Herlihy played in a feature film since coming to Hollywood. He had portrayed both Mark Twain and President Franklin D. Roosevelt, but never an Irishman.

Dan O'Herlihy jokingly told United Press International while promoting the film: "It's delicious. Cochran is a man who simply doesn't like children. I'm the father of five and the grandfather of four, so Cochran is a man with whom I can identify."

Nancy Loomis returns for her third appearance in a *Halloween* film as Linda Challis.

This film would mark the last series entry of John Carpenter, Debra Hill, Barry Bernardi and Dean Cundey from the franchise, all stalwarts from the original film.

The romance continues *further*: At the time of filming, Tom Atkins and Garn Stephens were married.

This film's central locale, Santa Mira, hails from *Invasion of the Body Snatchers*, which this film owes a great deal to.

The actual location used for Santa Mira was Loleta, California, a small town in the northern part of the state with a population of 738.

The facility used as the exterior of the Silver Shamrock factory was formerly the Familiar Foods factory in Loleta.

The gas station seen at the beginning and conclusion of this film was previously seen in *The Fog*.

Portions of the film were actually shot at Don Post's real life mask making factory.

Principal photography began on April 19, 1982, which was three hundred and sixty-six days after *Halloween II* began filming.

Halloween III's production was organized into a six-week shooting schedule.

An advertisement for the original *Halloween* plays on a television early in the film. A scene from the movie is later featured on the television in Dr. Challis' holding cell.

HALLOWEEN III

A significant number of the crickets used for Little Buddy's death scene eluded recapture by the special effects team. Their taking up residence in the hidden corners of the shooting space caused many a headache for the sound department on account of the cricket's incessant chirping.

The hotel registry that Dr. Challis scans for Harry Grimbrudge's name also features the names of several actual crewmembers including Costumer Frances Vega, Property Master James Rathbun and Script Supervisor Louise Jaffe.

Although Stacey Nelkin agreed to her character's love scene, she insisted upon a "no nipple" clause in her contract. As a result, Tommy Lee Wallace was forced to carefully shoot around this.

If Tom Atkins looked especially distressed or exhausted during filming, it might not necessarily owe to his performance. The actor came down with a bad case of the flu during production, but forged ahead anyway.

The "blood" spewed by Conal Cochran's robot army was actually frozen orange juice.

Garn Stephens stubbornly refused to wear makeup prosthetics for her character's death scene, requiring a body double to be used for the shot following the mask-chip blasting her face.

The famous shot in which a bound Dr. Challis successfully throws a mask overtop a security camera took forty takes to get right.

Tommy Lee Wallace both provided narration for the Silver Shamrock commercial and sang the actual song, the audio of which was then sped up.

If all of the cities included in the multi-city montage near the end of the film look similar, it is because they were almost all Los Angeles.

If the tune in the Silver Shamrock commercial seems familiar, it is because it uses a reworked version of *London Bridges Falling Down*, which was chosen for its public domain status. Noticing a pattern here?

The book Marge Gutman is seen reading before being zapped is "The Eagle's Gift" by Carlos Castaneda.

HALLOWEEN III

The producers turned to Burman Studios for the film's special effects needs. The effects shop boasts an impressive resume, both then and now, and also worked on another unfairly-maligned threequel: *The Godfather: Part III*.

The special effects budget on *Halloween III* was a tiny $25,000.

For the scene in which snakes and bugs pour out of Little Buddy's masked head, Burman Studios created a life-cast of actor Brad Schacter's upper torso and head. A mold was made from this casting and dressed as the character. The creepy crawlies were then fed out of the mask by a tube than ran through the prop.

More than 2,000 crickets were utilized for Little Buddy's death scene.

The snakebite on Buddy Senior's pants leg was filmed in reverse.

A portion of the score from *The Fog* can be heard over the radio in this film during a motel room scene.

The special effects team had four weeks to complete their work, three of which were prior to filming and one week once cameras had started rolling.

The scenes featuring the lab technician were not in the original script and only added after the film had been assembled.

The skull and witch masks featured in Silver Shamrock's lineup had been on sale by Don Post for several years prior to *Halloween III*. The pumpkin mask, however, was created exclusively for the film.

The song heard when the Kupfer's RV first pulls up is "Do the Boogaloo" by Quango and Sparky. The song was never commercially released to the public, though it was featured some years later in Christopher Nolan's *Memento*. It was not included on the film's soundtrack album.

The music heard over the radio just prior to Marge's "misfire" accident is the same music heard over the radio as Stevie drives to the lighthouse in *The Fog*.

John Carpenter and Alan Howarth teamed for their second and final *Halloween* movie score together.

HALLOWEEN III

Don Post Studios actually sold screen-accurate version of the three main masks from the movie complete with Silver Shamrock tags. When originally offered via mail-in, they were high-priced. When they eventually found their way into stores, they were considerably cheaper.

This marked the longest *Halloween* film up until this point at ninety-eight minutes long.

The film was sorely mis-advertised to the movie going public, most of who expected to see another movie about Michael Myers. The only indication whatsoever that it featured a different story was the inclusion of the words "All New" on some theatrical posters.

Poster artist Edd Riveria created the iconic artwork for this film's poster.

This film was nominated for a Saturn Award for Best Poster Art in 1983, but lost to John Alvin's *E.T.* poster.

Amazingly given the backlash, *Halloween III* managed to escape nomination for any of the 1982 Razzie Awards.

Halloween III opened on 1,250 theater screens on October 22, 1982.

Halloween III debuted alongside *First Blood*, which only barely beat it despite opening in four hundred fewer theaters. They would hold the first and second spots together at the box office on opening weekend and the following weekend. *Halloween III* slipped to eighth place its third weekend before vanishing from the top ten in its fourth weekend.

The film's box office take, which was $14.4 million, was disappointing to the studio in light of its potential. Universal then became disinterested in pursuing a *Halloween IV*.

The film featured as part of a promotion by Universal Pictures wherein kids that colored a *Halloween III* advertisement could earn free admission to the Universal Studios Tour with a paying adult. This was despite the fact that no part of *Halloween III* was actually filmed on the famed backlot. It was during this time period that Don Post Studios ran a mask-making demonstration as part of the tour.

Joe Dante caught the film in theaters upon release and spoke well of it. He also felt it was unfairly maligned by those wanting a direct sequel to *Halloween II*.

HALLOWEEN III

There are numerous bad reviews that could be quoted here, but this headline for Cinefantastique's was especially stinging since it was an actual genre magazine and not an ordinary movie publication: "Hack rewrite turns Kneale's treat into dreary chaos. Some trick." *Ouch.*

The film was turned into a novelization by Jack Martin, pen name for author Dennis Etchison. The author included numerous scenes and details not included in the film, including a reference to *Halloween II* reporter Robert Munday.

The 1986 trailer for Stephen King's *Maximum Overdrive*, which King personally hosted, overtly featured this film's main theme throughout. The eventual film did not.

Although I consider this film to be a perfectly respectable and enjoyable horror gem, I cannot help but giggle when I see people refer to it as *Halloween III: The Nap of Michael Myers*.

John Carpenter has maintained in recent years that he still enjoys this film, which is more than he says for *Halloween II*.

Despite her "no nipple" clause and seeming hesistance towards nudity, Stacey Nelkin later became a relationship and sex advice expert!

HALLOWEEN III

HALLOWEEN 4:
The Return of Michael Myers

Directed by Dwight Little

Written by Alan B. McElroy
Story by Alan B. McElroy, Larry Rattner, Dhani Lipsius
& Benjamin Ruffner

Donald Pleasance (Dr. Sam Loomis)
Danielle Harris (Jamie Lloyd)
Ellie Cornell (Rachel Carruthers)
Beau Starr (Sheriff Ben Meeker)
Kathleen Kinmont (Kelly Meeker)
Sasha Jenson (Brady)
George Wilbur (The Shape)

HALLOWEEN 4

This was the first *Halloween* sequel to be made without the involvement of Universal Pictures.

It was at Moustapha Akkad's insistence that this film return to the Michael Myers storyline of the first two films. Contrary to popular belief, the abandonment of the anthology franchise approach was not what originally drove John Carpenter and Debra Hill away from the series. In fact, they were (begrudgingly) on board with Michael's return.

John Carpenter originally teamed with Dennis Etchison to write a Michael Myers-centric *Halloween IV*. Their script focused on how traumatized Haddonfield had become following the first two films, eventually banning the Halloween holiday altogether. It was then through the attempted erasure of his legacy that Michael Myers (somehow) returned. Moustapha Akkad rejected the screenplay, calling it too cerebral.

Following the rejection of his script, John Carpenter sold his stake in the franchise along with Debra Hill to Moustapha Akkad, who sought a fresh start to *Halloween IV*.

Moustapha Akkad turned to the directing/writing team of Dwight H. Little and Alan B. McElroy, instructing them to return to the basics of the original *Halloween* rather than convolute the storyline or follow after the gory traditions of other slasher films.

Alan B. McElroy pitched and wrote the first draft of his screenplay in exactly eleven days in order to beat the looming Writer's Guild Strike. Screenwriter Sam Hamm did this also with Tim Burton's *Batman* for the same strike, submitting his script to Warner Brothers hours before it officially began.

This particular Writer's Strike would stand as the longest strike in the organization's long history at 155 days, ending in August. Had McElroy not have completed his draft, *Halloween IV* surely would have missed its projected October release date and been pushed to the following year, if not cancelled altogether.

This film inexplicably loses the Roman numeral number of the previous films to become *Halloween 4* rather than *Halloween IV*.

This film was made on a $5 million budget.

HALLOWEEN 4

This script continues the tradition of referring to Michael Myers in script direction as "The Shape."

Although this was not the directorial debut of director Dwight H. Little, it was his fourth film and the biggest production he had helmed yet.

Jamie Lloyd was originally named Brittany 'Briti' Carruthers. The was changed to Jamie in tribute to Jamie Lee Curtis.

Jamie Lloyd's dog, Sundae, is the third canine to be killed by Michael Myers. As a dog lover, I must ask… why in the hell are cats being spared in this franchise?

The brief part of Lindsey was originally going to be revealed as Lindsey Wallace from the first film.

The script initially called for Sheriff Meeker to be killed by Michael in his own basement, but not without putting up a fight first. Their battle would eventually cause the furnace to burn down the house, which meant the subsequent rooftop chase scene would have unfolded amid flames.

One idea envisioned for the schoolhouse scene involved Jamie hiding from Michael Myers under school desks. Briefly outsmarted, he would begin flipping over desks to find her. This abandoned concept was later used in *Halloween H20*.

While Dwight Little has commented that he did not dislike *Halloween III*, he felt it should not have worn the *Halloween* name.

Michael was originally scripted to encounter Jamie outside of the drugstore rather than only inside of it. The script called for his stolen tow truck to veer in front of Lindsey's car, prompting her to yell out at him not unlike Linda in the first *Halloween*.

The script cited the death of Laurie Strode's death as having happened eleven months prior. The film, however, states it as having occurred nine months prior.

The ambulance in the opening scenes was originally a prison bus.

Sabrina: The Teenage Witch star *Melissa* Joan Hart originally auditioned for the role of Jamie.

HALLOWEEN 4

While Michael Myer's middle name was mentioned as being Audrey in cut scenes for the first film, here Dr. Hoffman types it as having the initial "M" as in Michael M. Myers. This detail was not included in the shooting script, so it may possible have been the liberty of an overzealous set decorator rather than a continuity change-up.

Halloween 4 was originally scripted to begin with the ending of *Halloween II* in order to show Dr. Loomis being thrown far from the blast but still alive. As firefighters rushed to extinguish Michael's burning body, Loomis was to have yelled for them to "Let it burn!"

An early draft of the script saw Dr. Loomis originally traveling to Haddonfield to warn that Michael had returned home to finally kill Laurie Strode – unaware of her recent death.

Another early script draft saw "Evil Jamie" stab Rachel at the film's conclusion in place of her stepmother.

This film features but one returning cast member from the first two pictures: Donald Pleasance.

In a discarded line of dialogue, Earl and his redneck posse suspect terrorists as being responsible for the massacre at the police station.

Official promotional artwork released to *Variety* originally announced the film using the *IV* Roman numeral and misspelled the title character's last name as Meyers (as in it read *Halloween IV: The Return of Michael Meyers* when the title was, in fact, *Halloween 4: The Return of Michael Myers*.)

Total Body Count: 19 (including one dog).

Jamie Lee Curtis was offered the chance to return for this film, but declined. Her comedy-hit, *A Fish Called Wanda*, opened just prior to *Halloween IV*.

With Jamie Lee Curtis temporarily gone from the franchise, Pleasance's name is restored as the top-billed performer.

This production marks the film debut of future scream queen Danielle Harris.

Ellie Cornell was twenty-four at the time while her character was only "sixteen or seventeen," according to the script.

HALLOWEEN 4

Halloween 4 continued the practice started on *Halloween II* of hiring stuntmen to play Michael Myes with George Wilbur.

George Wilbur later revealed at various public appearances that he elected not to watch either of the first two *Halloween* movies prior to filming this one. He explained that he did not want the work of previous performerrs influencing his take on the character.

Mike Lookinland, better known to audiences as Bobby Brady on *The Brady Bunch*, was a production assistant on this film in his brief attempt to work behind the camera rather than in front of it. It was his last such job on a movie before returning to his most famous role that same year with *A Very Brady Christmas*.

Mike Lookinland's wife, Kelly, cameos as a dead waitress at the truck stop Michael slashes his way through. She later worked in the art department on *Halloween 5* and as script supervisor on *The Stand*, which borrowed locations from *Halloween 4*.

Ellie Cornell was originally offered the role of Alice in *Nightmare on Elm Street 4: The Dream Master*, but turned it down in order to appear in this film. The role of Alice was consequently written out of the franchise, never to appear in an *Elm Street* movie. (Not really… just curious to see if anyone is actually reading this!)

Up and coming actress Rebecca Schaeffer originally auditioned for the part of Rachel but lost out to Ellie Cornell. Schaeffer would be tragically murdered the following year by an obsessive stalker, prompting changes in California law to protect victims of stalking.

At the start of filming, Ellie Cornell had only seen parts of the original *Halloween* and neither of its sequels. Likewise, Danielle Harris was permitted to watch selections from the original film in order to prepare for her part as Jamie.

This film marks the first producorial appearance of Paul Freeman on the series.

Child actor Erik Preston originally auditioned to be one of the school children that taunts Jamie, but wound up being cast as Young Michael Myers instead.

HALLOWEEN 4

Despite playing a younger version of the titular character, Erik Preston's name does not appear in the credits. He is the third performer to portray young Michael.

Stuntman Tom Morga played a bandaged Michael Myers for scenes set at the truck stop as well as in the drugstore when he first acquires his new mask. He was not given credit for these scenes.

Tom Morga also stood in as Jason Voorhees (well, sort of) for several scenes in *Friday the 13th Part V: A New Beginning*. In a shitty turn of events, he also went uncredited for this role.

Both George Wilbur and Tom Morga stood at a towering 6'2, far and above the tallest performers up until then to portray Michael Myers.

Future producer Malek Akkad began his *Halloween* career on this film as a production assistant.

This was the first *Halloween* to depart Southern California for Salt Lake City, Utah.

The drugstore location in this film was later featured in Stephen King's *The Stand* and the family-comedy *The Sandlot*.

This was the first of only two Myers-centric *Halloween* films that do not feature the Myers House.

The script originally contained a throwaway line about the Myers House having been redesigned and put on the market, which would have explained its strange appearance in *Halloween 5* years before that director made the executive decision to ought ignore the franchise's architectural continuity.

Principal photography began on April 11, 1988.

This was the first film in the franchise to be shot in 1:85:1 aspect ratio and not the 2:35:1 seen on the first three pictures.

Writer Alan B. McElroy cameos as a state trooper at the ambulance crash site.

This is the first film in the franchise not to solely feature a close-up pumpkin for the opening credits.

HALLOWEEN 4

Danielle Harris turned eleven years old while filming the movie. She was given an on set party by the cast and crew.

Gaffer Garlan Wilde injured while hanging lights for the Michael/Brady confrontation when he fell from a ladder along with the light he was hanging, cutting his wrists.

Principal photography on this sequel lasted forty-one days.

Donald Pleasance was on set for ten of those days.

Danielle Harris and Ellie Cornell, however, were required to be onset for 34 and 36 of those days, respectively.

Erik Preston turned in three days of work on *Halloween 4*. The first two days were spent as an extra at Jamie's school and the final day as the vision of young Michael that Jamie sees in the drugstore mirror.

Danielle Harris' piercing screams for the running scene after Rachel falls from the roof were so alarming to local residents that multiple calls were placed to police insisting that a little girl was under attack.

The rooftop scene was not actually filmed several stories above the ground, but instead on a specially-built platform that was still somewhat high up. None of the performers wore safety harnesses.

Ellie Cornell incurred a nasty injury on the rooftop scene when she slid down onto a protruding nail. She was sent out to the local hospital for emergency stitches and returned to set that very same night to finish the scene.

George Wilbur, although tall, was not quite as large as the filmmakers originally wanted and consequently was required to wear hockey padding underneath his jumpsuit. This is particularly noticeable in some scenes.

George Wilbur made an effort to befriend Danielle Harris during filming and frequently removed his mask in front of her to keep from scaring her during their more intense scenes together.

Donald Pleasance not enthused over his character's new makeup appliance for the burns Dr. Loomis acquired in *Halloween II*, particularly the time it required him to spend in a makeup chair having it applied and removed.

HALLOWEEN 4

The scene in which Dr. Loomis discovers the ambulance wreckage was originally going to be far bloodier than it appeared in the finished film. The special effects department created a gaggle of dismembered body parts for the scene, none of which made the cut.

The box of photos that Michael discovers in Jamie's bedroom was originally going to contain an old photo of him and Judith on Halloween night, 1963 mere hours before his first murder.

Legendary effectsman John Carl Buechler provided special effects on this film. He had only recently wrapped production on *Friday the 13th Part VII: The New Blood*, which he directed.

It was decided after the first cut of the film had been assembled that *Halloween 4* had barely earned its R-rating and needed additional gore content. Consequently, John Carl Buechler was commissioned to direct several days of "blood filming" with a second unit that included Michael's thumb jamming into the ambulance tech's forehead and the redneck's neck being ripped open.

Although *Halloween 4* marks Alan Howarth's third time scoring a *Halloween* movie, it is actually his first time doing it solo.

In addition to not featuring a pumpkin close-up in its opening credits, this is the first *Halloween* filmed not to feature John Carpenter's main theme over the opening titles.

1988 was a particularly big year for horror. Not only did it see the theatrical return of Michael Myers but also big screen appearances from the *Friday the 13th* and *Nightmare on Elm Street* franchises as well.

The theatrical posters for both this film and *Halloween 5* are somewhat misleading. This sequel's poster inexplicably features the Wallace house from the original *Halloween* despite it not appearing in the film itself. Similarly, the poster's Michael Myers mask is clearly based on the original and not the replacement one used throughout this film.

Halloween 4 opened on 1,679 theater screens.

The film opened in the top spot at the box office with a $6.8 million opening weekend. It remained there the following weekend as well.

HALLOWEEN 4

The sequel's total domestic box office gross was $17.9 million.

Ellie Cornell and Sasha Jensen (Brady) both appeared in an ABC Afterschool Special following their time together in *Halloween 4*.

Danielle Harris was allowed to keep her clown costume from the film. She eventually sold it to a *Halloween* fan.

Halloween 4 was the first sequel to actually put Michael Myers on the cover of Fangoria magazine with issue #79. Fangoria did not exist when the first *Halloween* came out and the issue covering *Halloween II* featured the pumpkin artwork rather than Michael's pale visage. Strangely, the magazine's 79th issue highlighting Michael's long awaited return to the big screen featured –of all things – a pullout poster of a disfigured Marge Gutman from *Halloween III*. Because who hasn't wanted to hang that particular image on their bedroom wall?

HALLOWEEN 5:
The Revenge of Michael Myers

Directed by Dominique Othenin-Girard

Written by Dominique Othenin-Girard, Michael Jacobs & Shem Bitterman

Donald Pleasance (Dr. Sam Loomis)
Danielle Harris (Jamie Lloyd)
Ellie Cornell (Rachel Carruthers)
Beau Starr (Sheriff Ben Meeker)
Jeffrey Landman (Billy Hill)
Tamara Glynn (Samantha Thomas)
Jonathan Chaplin (Mikey)
Matthew Walker (Spitz)
Don Shanks (The Shape)

HALLOWEEN 5

Dennis Etchinson, who novelized *Halloween II* and *III* under a pen name, actually made reference to *Halloween 5* in his 1986 novel *Darkside* This novel was released before *Halloween 4* had even been green lit.

Rushed into production before the script had been perfected. Moustapha Akkad has since often claimed to have been "drunk" off the success of *Halloween 4* when he made this movie.

Although not officially involved with *Halloween 5*, Debra Hill was the person responsible for recommending Dominique Othenin-Girard.

Dominique Othenin-Girard, arguably a poor choice for director. Swiss-French speaking.

To prepare for this film, Dominique Othenin-Girard claims to have watched all entries of the *Halloween, Friday the 13th* and *Nightmare on Elm Street* franchises available to him at that time.

No script draft of this film carries the *Revenge of Michael Myers* subtitle. Several drafts did contain an alternate subtitle, however. It read: *Halloween 5… and Things that Go Bump in the Night.*"

This film marks the second time in the franchise Michael Myers has been unmasked onscreen, the first time having occurred in the original *Halloween*.

This film's budget was $3 million.

Shem Bitterman originally wrote a script for this film that built upon *Halloween 4*'s idea of Jamie Lloyd becoming evil. A handful of series veterans were enthusiastic about this approach including Daniele Harris and Donald Pleasance. Dominique Othenin-Girard, however, hated this draft and defiantly threw it into a trashcan during a meeting with Moustapha Akkad. He was then allowed to re-write the script with Michael Jacobs.

Although Shem Bitterman remains a credited writer on the film, no element from his script made it to the screen.

Dominique Othenin-Girard has repeated over the years that he sought to humanize Michael Myers in this sequel.

HALLOWEEN 5

The script consistently misspells Michael's last name as Meyers.

It also misspells Carruthers as Caruthers.

In one of only a few callbacks to the original *Halloween*, this script continues the tradition of referring to Michael as "The Shape" in screen direction.

It was originally written that Tina's costume was to be "Queen of Outer Space," essentially a bikini.

This film marks the third time that Michael has pretended to be someone's boyfriend. He previously pretended to be Bob in *Halloween* and Bud in *Halloween II*.

The Man in Black was created in order to setup *Halloween 6* at Moustapha Akkad's request. The character was made intentionally vague so that the next filmmaking team, which Dominique Othenin-Girard initially envisioned himself as being part of, could write his story for that film. When Dominique Othenin-Girard departed the series after this film, whatever ideas he had about the role went with him.

The film's shooting script contains perhaps the most bizarre note ever included in a horror film script. Just before the sex scene in the barn, Dominique Othenin-Girard writes: "Director's Note" This scene will be filmed with all the gentleness necessary to give adolescents a good feeling about their first time."

Dominique Othenin-Girard felt that by killing off Rachel early in the film he would be shaking the audience's assumptions about who could live and die.

Max becomes the fourth dog Michael kills in this franchise. Seriously, why are freaking cats being spared here?

Total Body Count: 10 not counting the police massacre

Don Shanks, who was chosen to play Michael, was then perhaps best known as Nakoma on *The Life and Times of Grizzly Adams*.

Unlike his predecessor, Don Shanks did not need padding to appear large. He was 6'1.

Don Shanks also portrayed the mysterious Man in Black.

HALLOWEEN 5

Although Don Shanks had already seen the first two *Halloween* films at his time of hire, he was instructed by the director *not* to watch any of the preceding films or to study the Michael's that had come before him.

Donald Pleasance, Danielle Harris, Ellie Cornell and Beau Starr return from *Halloween 4*.

Donald Pleasance was candidly vocal, even in publicity, for the sequel about his displeasure over *Halloween 5* "wasting" the rich opportunities that *Halloween 4* had set up for its successor.

This was the first *Halloween* to feature original footage from *two* Halloween nights (both 1988 and 1989 are seen in this film.)

Jeff Landman claims to have only watched *Halloween III* prior to shooting this film, as *Halloween 4* was not yet available on home video. Being that part *III* did not contain Michael Myers, he walked onto set very confused on the first day of filming.

Ellie Cornell was not pleased to read that Rachel was to be killed off so early into the film, especially by getting a pair of scissors rammed down her throat. The scene was toned down at her request.

Like its predecessor, this film lensed in Salt-Lake City.

This sequel features a considerably different looking Myers House, not because the production team could not find a convincing duplicate in Salt Lake City, but because Dominique Othenin-Girard wanted a house that fit scenes he had written into the script. This was apparently easier than simply writing a script that fit inside of pre-existing continuity with regard to a major series location.

The drugstore from *Halloween 4* is briefly visible when the Man in Black steps off the bus.

And the romance continues *again:* Wendy Kaplan was dating Greg Nicotero throughout filming of this movie.

Halloween 5 began filming on May 1, 1989.

The shooting schedule was front-loaded with Donald Pleasance's scenes first. After his ten days of filming, he

HALLOWEEN 5

reportedly spoke to the producers about letting Danielle Harris use his more luxurious trailer on set.

After *Halloween 4*'s different (but terrific) opening sequence, this film returns to the familiar pumpkin-motif opening of previous films.

The laundry chute scene was mostly filmed laying horizontally flat rather than vertically.

The filmmakers asked that KNB Effects design a facial makeup for Michael's unmasking scene in case they decided to use it. They opted against using it and Michael's skin appears both unscarred and clean... you know... for the scene in which he cries.

Michael Myers goddamn cries in this movie.

The actual shot of Michael Myer's crying was done in extreme close-up. Such a shot requires enormous precision from both the subject and the camera operators. As such, Don Shanks was required to strap his head into a brace to prevent him from moving out of focus and/or frame.

Fortunately, the stuntman was also an actor and able to cry on cue so that no fake tears were needed from the makeup department.

The bumbling cops and their accompany clown music were an homage to similar characters in Wes Craven's *The Last House on the Left*.

Jeff Landman was allowed to keep his character's pirate costume from filming and still has it to this day.

The look of the Man in Black changed sometime between writing and production. He was described in the script as having an "Italian cut suit" when fist introduced, though the film takes clear inspiration from Johnny Cash's persona of the same name.

For the scene in which Dr. Loomis yells into the woods at Michael Myers, Donald Pleasance requested that Don Shanks actually stand amongst the darkness to help motivate his performance. This was despite Don Shanks having already wrapped his work for the evening and not having been scheduled for the scene in question. Ever a good sport, Shanks happily complied with his co-stars request.

HALLOWEEN 5

In between filming, Beau Starr recorded a bizarre promotional spot for the film as Sheriff Meeker where he swears his own revenge against Michael Myers. Although the spot appears as bonus material on home video releases of the film, it was never actually used to market the movie.

Donald Pleasance reportedly broke Don Shank's nose (accidentally, of course) while filming the climactic beat down scene.

Car fans rest easy... the Camaro Michael damages during Spitz' death scene was not actually damaged. A faux-covering was put over the actual car to prevent any nicks or scratches.

Although it is not clearly spelled out in the film, it was originally thought that Dr. Loomis would have died upon collapsing onto Michael at the end. Consequently, Donald Pleasance told multiple media outlets that *Halloween 5* would have to be his last since his character finally died in it.

The sequel's ending unfolds differently in the script issued just prior to filming. Rather than capturing Michael with a net, Dr. Loomis rigs the staircase to break beneath Michael's feet. He would then have dropped into a cage planted before the confrontation. The subsequent scene inside Michael's jail cell would have also unfolded differently. He was not to have been sitting quietly, but raging against the metal bars so hard that they start to bend outward.

The filmmakers shot the jail cell scene at the end twice, once with Michael wearing his mask and once without the mask. They eventually chose to leave his mask on, despite this being highly illogical from a police procedural standpoint.

Dramatically different mask with regard to eye holes, hair and the massive neck flap.

Michael was originally to don a Ronald Regan mask for the scene in which he drives Tina, but the producers didn't want it to be mistaken for a political statement.

Dominique Othenin-Girard wanted considerably more blood and gore in this sequel while also wanting to return to the simplicity of the original *Halloween*, concepts that were in enormous conflict with one another.

The mask was mold-fitted to Don Shank's face by KNB FX

HALLOWEEN 5

Although the film was widely marketed as having the *Revenge of Michael Myers* subtitle, the film's title card simply reads *Halloween 5*.

This would be the last *Halloween* sequel to carry a number in its title until Rob Zombie's *Halloween II* (2009).

Galaxy International marketed this film with a 1-900 number wherein callers could attempt to save Michael's next victim by pressing buttons (as in "Press 1 to hide in the attic or 2 to hide in the bedroom").

This film's theatrical poster, like its predecessor's poster, is somewhat misleading. It features Jamie Lloyd wearing her clown costume from *Halloween 4*, though she does not wear it in this film unless you count the several seconds of *Halloween 4* flashback that open the movie. Rather in this film she wears a ballerina costume. Furthermore, the Michael Myers mask seen on the *Halloween 5* poster bears no resemblance to the neck-flapping mask seen in the actual movie.

Halloween 5 was released on October 13, 1989. This is the earliest date upon which a *Halloween* had yet been released. The franchise's fifth installment opened on 1,495 screens.

The sequel opened against the original *Look Who's Talking*, which bested it for the #1 spot at the box office. At second place, *Hallowen 5*'s opening weekend take was $5.1 million. It dropped to sixth the following weekend before disappearing from the top ten films.

The domestic box office take amounted to $11.6 million.

The film was not well received outside of North American and went direct-to-video in nearly every foreign market.

This was the first *Halloween* film not to receive a novelization, though Nicholas Grabowsky later volunteered to write adaptations of both this and *Halloween 6*.

Upon reflecting on the mistakes of *Halloween 5*, Moustapha Akkad vowed to never rush another sequel into production. He decided a period of at least two years between sequels was necessary for adequate development and so that home video releases and theatrical releases did not compete with one another.

BEHIND THE SCENES OF THE HALLOWEEN MOVIES

HALLOWEEN 5

HALLOWEEN:
THE CURSE OF MICHAEL MYERS

Directed by Joe Chappelle

Written by Daniel Farrands

Donald Pleasance (Dr. Sam Loomis)
Paul Rudd (Tommy Doyle)
Marianne Hagan (Kara Strode)
Mitchell Ryan (Dr. Terrance Wynn)
Kim Darby (Debra Strode)
Bradford English (John Strode)
Keith Bogart (Tim Strode)
J.C. Brandy (Jamie Lloyd)
George Wilbur (The Shape)

HALLOWEEN 6

Halloween 5's Dominique Othenin-Girard had originally intended to write and direct *Halloween 6* himself and continue the plot threads he had begun with the Man in Black storyline. He eventually left the project due to creative differences with Moustapha Akkad and took with him the original story elements for the character.

The eventual script for *Halloween*'s sixth was written by a longtime horror fan by the name of Daniel Farrands. At the time he was hired, Farrands had but one other feature film writing credit to his name.

Daniel Farrands differentiated himself from other writers pitching their take on the sequel by having done extensive research on the Thorn symbol and by building upon the mythology started in *Halloween 5*.

What ultimately set Daniel Farrands apart from other writers was that he was a true fan of the franchise, not simply a writer-for-hire. Seriously, the guy knows and loves his *Halloween*. If he were to cut his finger on something sharp, his blood would bleed orange. That's how hardcore he is.

The film's original script was a smart one that connected back to the original *Halloween* on multiple levels. It was unfortunately mangled and rewritten by the director and others into the film we have today. Few of Daniel Farrand's ideas reached the big screen as originally intended.

This film addresses Dr. Loomis' apparent demise at the end of *Halloween 5* by referring to his collapse onto Michael Myers as a stroke instead.

Script drafts refer to the film as *Halloween 666* while early marketing materials call it *Halloween 666: The Origin of Michael Myers*. The official name the studio eventually went with dropped the number to simply become *Halloween: The Curse of Michael Myers*.

This was the first sequel made by Dimension Films.

Dimension Films had previously found success creating profitable sequels to well-known genre properties including *Hellraiser*, *Children of the Corn* and *Highlander*.

The film was originally budgeted at $5 million, though more than $1 million was slashed at the last moment and given to another Dimension Films production.

HALLOWEEN 6

Fred Walton, who had directed slasher-classics *When a Stranger Calls* and *April Fool's Day*, was originally attached to direct the film. He would retire from filmmaking shortly after departing this film.

Joe Chappelle was hired to replace Dominique Othenin-Girard. Like the film's screenwriter, Chappelle had but one feature film directing credit to his name before boarding this project. He has since disowned this film, refusing to discuss it or make public appearances related to it, likely in an effort to avoid the first public stoning since the biblical age.

Joe Chappelle strongly disliked *Halloween 5* and removed several originally planned references to it including the police station flashback originally intended to open this film.

Additionally, rumors emanated from the film's set that Joe Chappelle found Donald Pleasance boring…. Or as Daniel Farrands put it in an interview with HalloweenMovies.com, felt that he "slowed the pace of the film.")

This film resurrects two otherwise forgotten characters from the first *Halloween* with Dr. Wynn and Tommy Doyle. Tommy had originally been considered for inclusion in *Halloween 4* before being dropped.

An early script draft resurrected not only Tommy from the original film, but Lindsey Wallace as well. Audiences would have found the two now a couple hunting Michael together.

Daniel Farrands has cited *Rosemary's Baby* as being an influence on this sequel. The 1968 film was originally going to be referenced in dialogue by radio host Barry Sims.

Daniel Farrands lobbied to have Christopher Lee cast as Dr. Wynn since the performer had regretfully passed on the Loomis role in the original *Halloween*. The filmmakers were disinterested, however, and went with Mitch Ryan instead.

Kara being chased across the street and banging on the door of Ms. Blankenship's home was meant to evoke a similar scene in the original *Halloween*.

Debra Strode's death amongst the drying sheets was also an homage to the original film where Michael watched Laurie from and then disappeared among the drying sheets.

HALLOWEEN 6

Characters John and Debra Strode are named in tribute to series creators John Carpenter and Debra Hill.

In an attempt to bridge the films together, Daniel Farrands included a character named Ms. Blankenship, who is later revealed to have babysat Michael Myers as a young boy. In *Halloween III*, Ellie mentions her father as having an appointment with Ms. Blankenship.

The original script included another more direct *Halloween III* reference as well. The film was to be playing on television when John Strode arrived home on Halloween night. This detail was not realized in the film.

The "stomach pounder" beverage Tim Strode jokes about is a reference to John Carpenter's *The Fog*.

Daniel Farrands advocated strongly for the return of the Jamie Lloyd character and for her to survive until the final act in which she would heroically die fighting Michael Myers. While he was allowed to write this into a draft, the part was subsequently scaled back down after Danielle Harris left the production.

Total Body Count: 20 (ish)

This film marks the big screen debut of Paul Rudd. Although he appeared on theater screens first in 1995's *Clueless*, he had actually filmed his *Halloween 6* material before filming that movie.

James Parks, Michael Worth and Christopher Daniel Barnes were all considered for the role of Tommy before Paul Rudd was cast.

In a move that proves the wrong people were making decisions on *Halloween 6*, Danielle Harris was not invited back to appear in this film. It was only upon suggesting herself that she was able to meet with the filmmakers. She was not happy with the script or how Jamie was to be killed and requested changes be made. She was further appalled by the paltry pay rate she was offered by the production company to reprise her most famous role. The combination of her dislike for the script and the insulting pay led to her not returning to the role of Jamie Lloyd.

Wendy Benson-Landes auditioned for the role of Kara Strode but was turned down by producers. She went on to appear in Robert Kurtzman's *Wishmaster* shortly thereafter.

HALLOWEEN 6

Marianne Hagan was very nearly not cast as Kara Strode. Studio heads worried her chin might be "too pointy" and her body "too thin" for the part. Knowledge of this led to her feeling insecure about her casting during filming.

Shock jock Barry Sims was based on shock jock Howard Stern, whom the filmmakers approached to play the role. Stern declined, however, wanting to focus his energies on both his show and his own film, *Private Parts*, which was then in development.

Once again, Donald Pleasance is the only returning actor from the previous film.

Denise Richards auditioned for the role of Beth, but was rejected.

Moustapha Akkad personally invited *Halloween 4's George* Wilbur back to play Michael Myers. This made him the only performer to have played the role twice in the franchise up until Tyler Mane.

Brian Andrews, who played Tommy Doyle in the original *Halloween*, was none too pleased that he was recast in this film. He has sharply rebuffed claims by the filmmakers that they were unable to locate him because he seldom acted anymore, citing that his contact information has been on file with the Screen Actors Guild for decades. Andrews claims to have never watched this sequel because of his snub.

This film has two John Wayne connections. Kim Darby was well known as starring in the original *True Grit* alongside the Duke. George Wilbur also began his career standing-in for John Wayne.

This sequel features a new location for the Myers House, ditching the gothic castle from the previous film, however it still does not evoke the original house from the first two *Halloween* films.

For the first time since *Halloween II*, the Myers House is seen as existing at 45 Lampkin Lane.

This sequel marks the first trip back to Smith's Grove - Warren County Sanitarium since the original *Halloween*. Michael Myers was supposed to be transferred here at the start of *Halloween 4*, but escaped while en route.

HALLOWEEN 6

This is the third and final sequel to film in Salt Lake City.

The real-life location used for the exteriors of Smith's Grove Sanitarium in this film was previously seen as Ridgemont Federal Sanitarium in *Halloween 4*. It is now an upscale condominium complex... so if you have ever wanted to live where Michael spent so many formative years, you now can!!

The hospital used for interior reshoots on *Halloween 6* was Queen of Angels Hospital in Los Angeles where *The Propehcy* also filmed. This location has a number of its own ghost stories and has since been turned into The Dream Center hospital.

If Ms. Blankenship was a cult member in 1963, it is entirely possible (retroactively, of course!) that the opening shot from *Halloween* is of Michael Myers leaving her house to kill his sister.

Although not clearly stated in the Producer's Cut itself, Jamie Lloyd is taken to Haddonfield Memorial Hospital, last seen in *Halloween II*.

Filming began on October 28, 1994.

This would be the first *Halloween* in the franchise's history to actually shoot on the holiday of Halloween.

This film was being made concurrent with *Hellraiser: Bloodline*, also from Dimension Films. Director Kevin Yagher eventually quit the project and disowned the film over creative disputes with the studio. It has been strongly rumored that Dimension siphoned more than $1 million from the budget of *Halloween 6* for extensive reshoots on *Bloodline*, which they entrusted to Joe Chappelle. The *Hellraiser* sequel that resulted was a mangled disaster that neither director took credit for.

This film seen playing on Ms. Blankenship's television is the original silent *Phantom of the Opera*. The original joke was going to be that Ms. Blankenship, being old and hard of hearing, would choose to watch a *silent* movie on television.

One of the *Haddonfield Star Ledger* prop newspapers that litters Tommy's room features a picture of Danielle Harris with the headline: "Myers' Niece Presumed Dead."

HALLOWEEN 6

George Wilbur had since "shaped" up (or out) physically and no longer required the hockey padding he needed when playing Michael Myers in *Halloween 4*.

Daniel Farrands was present during filming and documented production with his own home video camera.

The production ran into problems around the predominantly Mormon Salt Lake City when they announced their film as *Halloween 666*. They very quickly learned to call themselves something else when dealing with the local population.

Salt Lake City experienced an unusually early winter in 1994 and it snowed a considerable amount, forcing the production indoors.

The sequel's title began to change during filming after the production company started to receive letters from distributors fearing that Christian filmgoers might not see a film with *666* in its title. It was only then that Daniel Farrands jokingly suggested *The Curse of Michael Myers* on account of how cursed the production seemed at the time. Moustapha Akkad liked it and went with it.

The radio station that broadcasts the Barry Sims Show has WKNB for their call letters, an obvious reference to KNB Effects.

The film's electronic press kit, which was distributed to media outlets across the country, featured behind-the-scenes footage captured from scenes only included in the Producer's Cut, much to the confusion of fans paying attention at home.

Donald Pleasance passed away unexpectedly shortly after principal photography was completed on February 2nd, 1995. He would therefore not be available for reshoots, which were written around material he had already filmed.

George Wilbur was unavailable for some of the film's extensive reshoots. He was replaced under the mask by A. Michael Lerner, whose father, Fred, had coordinated stunts on *Halloween 5*. Fred appears in *Halloween 6* as the doctor Michael kills in the tunnel, essentially meaning that A. Michael Lerner killed his father onscreen.

Much of the film's gore content such as Jamie being shredded by farm equipment and John Strode's head exploding came during reshoots at the request of the studio.

HALLOWEEN 6

Donald Pleasance disliked having to wear a burned makeup appliance on *Halloween 4* and *5*. This prompted the filmmakers to write into their film an explanation for him appearing normal – a skin graft surgery.

The original, discarded cut of the film, which much more closely reflected the script, was known as "The Producer's Cut," and widely circulated as a bootleg work print in the years that followed.

The original cut tested poorly with audiences, a process previous sequels had not been subject to. Unhappy with the film themselves, Joe Chappelle and filmmaking partner Rand Ravich rewrote and refilmed almost the entire third act of the movie into what is now seen in the theatrical version of the film.

Alan Howarth again returned to score the film. When the film went back into production for reshoots, Howarth was ordered to create new score material. The rock-guitar *Halloween* theme was included in the film at Joe Chappelle's request.

This film received an NC-17 rating when first submitted to the MPAA. Subsequent edits allowed to to be released with only an R-rating.

The soundtrack features several songs from Alabama rock-band Brother Kane, notably *And Fools Shine On*, which featured into the film itself as well as its marketing. (These guys are pretty good at what they do – so give them a listen once you put this book down.)

The filmmakers staged a continuation of *Halloween 5*'s ending using a photo double for young Danielle Harris. It was eventually cut by Joe Chappelle due to his dislike for all things *Halloween 5*.

This film is dedicated to the memory of Donald Pleasance.

The film opened on September 29, 1995, which was then the earliest a *Halloween* film had opened.

It opened on 1,679 theater screens.

The soundtrack eventually released by Varèse Sarabande was a seemingly random collection of music from both the theatrical and producer's cuts of the film.

HALLOWEEN 6

It debuted second at the box office with $7.3 million, unable to topple *Seven*. It dropped to eighth place the following weekend (*Seven* remained in the top spot) before disappearing from the top ten altogether.

Domestically, the film grossed more than $15 million.

With this film, the *Halloween* series now mirrored successive titles from the *Pink Panther* series, which also featured a *Return/Revenge/Curse* trilogy. (*Return of the Pink Panther*, *Revenge of the Pink Panther* and *Curse of the Pink Panther*.) It remains to be seen whether or not we get a *Trail of Michael Myers* or *Michael Myers Strikes Again* a la the *Pink Panther*.

Paul Rudd later told Capone of *Ain't it Cool News* that while his experience making *Halloween 6* was good, he felt the film itself was not. He did have many good things to say about the production, however.

On September 23, 2014, hell literally froze over and pigs took flight when Shout Factory released a restored version of the Producer's Cut onto Blu-Ray.

HALLOWEEN H20
TWENTY YEARS LATER

Directed by Steve Miner

Written by Robert Zappia & Matt Greenberg
Story by Robert Zappia

Jamie Lee Curtis (Laurie Strode/Keri Tate)
Adam Arkin (Will Brennan)
Josh Hartnett (John Tate)
Michelle Williams (Molly Cartwell)
Adam Hann-Byrd (Charles Deveraux)
Jodi Lyn O'Keefe (Sarah Wainthrope)
LL Cool J (Ronny Jones)
Chris Durand (The Shape)

HALLOWEEN H20

This film was initially developed as a direct-to-video sequel to be written by Robert Zappia His first draft predated the participation of Jamie Lee Curtis.

Jamie Lee Curtis came on board the project hoping to create a "love letter" to her fan base in the form of a twentieth anniversary sequel. She initially met with John Carpenter and Debra Hill about working on the film.

John Carpenter actually entertained the idea of returning to the franchise, but only for a steep director's fee to make up for both his disinterest in the property and profits he felt he had missed out on over the years. His fee was immediately rejected and he departed the sequel.

Kevin Williamson penned an early treatment for this film, very little of which ended up in the finished film. While he was instrumental in developing the project, he did not actually write enough to qualify for co-writer status by Writer's Guild standards. As a result, he was given an Executive Producer credit instead.

Kevin Williamson spoke publicly about liking *Halloween 4* and parts of *Halloween 5*, but feeling that *Halloween 6* failed the series.

One early working title for the film was *Halloween 7: The Revenge of Laurie Strode*.

Steve Miner boarded the film having worked with Jamie Lee Curtis before on *Forever Young*. He was also no stranger to the horror genre having directed the first two sequels to *Friday the 13th*.

Near the end of the film, Keri Tate tells the fleeing students to drive to the Becker's house to call the police. This not only evokes a similar scene from the first *Halloween*, it references *Scream* in that Drew Barrymore's character from the first film was named Casey Becker.

An early script draft saw Rachel Loomis, Sam's apparent daughter, in the place of Marion Whittington in the opening.

This is the first Michael Myers-related *Halloween* film in the franchise not to take place in Haddonfield.

HALLOWEEN H20

While this film infamously (and perhaps notoriously to some fans) ignores the continuity of films *4, 5* and *6*, it was originally intended to make passing acknowledgment of it. One of Keri's students was to read aloud a report in class about the 'Haddonfield Murders" of the past two decades. At the very mention of Jamie Lloyd's name, an unsettled Keri Tate was to bolt from the class toward the bathroom to throw up.

This film boasted a $17 million budget, far and above the highest in the franchise.

The film's eventual title, *Halloween H20*, is meant to stand for *Halloween Twenty Years Later*. It also works on a scientific level. The pH Balance of water is very close to 7.0.

Total Body Count: 7

This film marked the feature film debut of Josh Hartnett.

Jamie Lee Curtis's mother, Janet Leigh, came out of retirement to appear in this film alongside her daughter. It marked her first theatrical film appearance in eighteen years.

This marked the second time Jamie Lee Curtis and Janet Leigh appeared together in a John Carpenter-related production. The first was 1980's *The Fog*.

Kane Hodder, famous for playing Jason Voorhees in four of the *Friday the 13th* films, auditioned to play Michael Myers in this film but was rejected by producers.

PJ Soles was originally sought after for the role of Keri Tate's secretary. Supposedly, she was not enthusiastic over the part and soon passed over when Janet Leigh expressed interest in the role.

That Janet Leigh's character was named Norma was not happenstance. It is a reference to Norman Bates from *Psycho* in which she became the screen's first Scream Queen through her murder in the shower.

Charles S. Dutton of *Alien 3* and *Gothika* fame was originally cast as a detective tracking Michael Myers in a sub-plot excised three weeks before filming began.

Jamie Lee Curtis was originally an advocate of detective sub-plot (the so-called "B" story of the film), but trusted Steve Miner's decision to focus instead solely on the Keri

HALLOWEEN H20

Tate storyline. She has since agreed with his decision. If *Halloween H20* feels lacking at all – it may be due to the fact that its story was slashed in this manner.

Michelle Williams had not seen a *Halloween* film prior to appearing in this one.

When Adam-Hann Byrd was first cast as Charlie, he was to have been revealed as a copycat killer imitating Michael Myers. Shortly after his reveal, the actual Michael was to have appeared and killed him.

As part of her contractual agreement on *Halloween H20*, Jamie Lee Curtis agreed to make a limited cameo at the start of the next *Halloween* sequel to conclude her character's storyline.

Although she had known of him for decades, Jamie Lee Curtis had never actually met Moustapha Akkad in person until preproduction on *Halloween H20*.

Jamie Lee Curtis maintains she never saw *Halloween 4, 5* or *6*.

This film features no returning cast from *Halloween: The Curse of Michael Myers*. The only returning cast members featured at all are Jamie Lee Curtis and Nancy Stephens, both of whom were last seen in *Halloween II*.

A handful of *Halloween H20* cast members belonged to ongoing television series at the time of filming. Adam Arkin was on *Chicago Hope*. Joseph Gordon-Levitt was still appearing on *3rd Rock from the Sun*. Michelle Williams was just beginning *Dawson's Creek*. Even LL Cool J was a regular on *In the House*.

The film's central Northern California setting of Summer Glenn is fictional not unlike Haddonfield.

The Canfield-Moreno Estate in Los Angeles, which served as the Hillcrest Academy in *Halloween H20*, was later seen in *Scream 3*.

This is the first series entry to be filmed in California since *Halloween III* and the first-ever to be set there.

Part of the film was also shot on Stage 24 at Universal Studios Hollywood.

HALLOWEEN H20

This film mentions Marion as living on Cypress Pond Road. Jamie Lee Curtis' character in Steve Miner's *Forever Young* lives on the same fictional road.

Principal photography began on February 7, 1998.

The film's workprint features *So I Married an Axe Murderer* on Sarah and Molly's television in a humorous nod to that film's star (Mike Myers name often being confused for Michael Myers). The theatrical version of the film, however, shows *Scream 2* playing on television.

Chris Durand also portrayed the Ghostface killer in *Scream 2* for several stunt scenes.

As often happens in these films, *Scream 2* seemingly jumps ahead between shots.

Steve Miner cameos as the school's financial advisor talking to Molly when we first meet her character.

The film playing on television in the opening scene is *Plan 9 from Outer Space*.

Universal Studios let the production borrow the car Janet Leigh's character drove in *Psycho* for her final scene in *Halloween H20*.

In their Story Notes presentation of the film, American Movie Classics notes: "The last time Janet Leigh rode in this car, it was in the trunk."

A *Halloween: The Curse of Michael Myers* publicity photo of Donald Pleasance appears in a newspaper clipping during the opening credits sequence.

A crime scene photo of bloody scissors can also be seen in the opening credits sequence, possibly in reference to Rachel's death in *Halloween 5*.

The restaurant scene where Will leaves the table and Keri downs her glass of wine before sharply ordering another is common among alcoholics as a way to hide their addiction. When Will returns to the table, it will appear to him as though Keri is still on her previous glass when she is, in fact, at least one glass ahead.

This film has the longest pre-title sequence of any *Halloween* up until then – nearly 11 minutes.

HALLOWEEN H20

While *Halloween H20* has several deleted scenes, the filmmakers also captured several shots for use only in marketing the film such as Jodi Lyn O'Keefe screaming outside at night and a close-up of Jamie Lee Curtis yelling for Michael with the axe.

One of the clippings in Dr. Loomis' office shows a yearbook photo with Laurie Strode and reads "Class of 1978." This is a goof, however, as Laurie would have been the class of 1979 if she was a senior in October 1978.

LL Cool J had something big in common with his character – they were both writers. In the film, Ronnie is trying to complete a new erotic fiction novella. In reality, LL Cool J was finishing his own autobiography while filming *Halloween H20*.

Halloween II's Dick Warlock told the *Gorehound Mike* blog he was called on this film to potentially replace Chris Durand, but that he thought the production truly only wanted his original *Halloween/Halloween II* mask.

Entertainment Weekly noted in their set report that Jamie Lee Curtis gave her mother an "I Survived Halloween" present on her last day of shooting in the form of a gumball machine filled with candy corns. Janet Leigh was quick to point out that this was Norman's favorite snack in *Psycho*, which Curtis claims to have been entirely coincidental.

Although not included in the shooting script, a loophole was devised mid-production to allow for Michael Myers to return in *Halloween 8*. This was created and filmed at the request of Moustapha Akkad who never intended to end the franchise with this installment.

One memorable image from the film that Jamie Lee Curtis had hoped would become the theatrical poster artwork was the shot of Michael Myers peering through the bathroom stall door at the rest stop.

In Chris Durand's opinion, the most dangerous stunt he performed in the film was the van-wreck at the end.

Michael Myers was originally scripted to speak one word as he lay pinned beneath the wrecked van. He was to look at his sister and speak her name ("Laurie") with arms outstretched. This was cut out concurrent with the creation of a loophole

HALLOWEEN H20

to allow for *Halloween 8*, which was that Michael was *not* under the mask at that moment. Chris Durand has since voiced his support for Michael not speaking in the film.

Jamie Lee Curtis gave a lengthy interview in her daytime Keri Tate costume on the schoolroom set that was used in bonus material on several *Halloween* home video releases as well as in A&E's *Halloween: The Inside Story*.

One of the biggest controversies surrounding this film involved the handful of masks used during production.

As a result of the mask controversy, Adam Arkin had to reshoot his death scene due to the introduction of a new mask to the production.

The introductory pan-down shot that introduces Hillcrest Academy features computer-generated buildings where in reality only trees exist. The birds that fly by are also computer-generated.

Rather than lift audio from the original *Halloween*, the filmmakers brought in voice actor Tom Kane to re-record

Donald Pleasance's lines as Dr. Loomis, which he did fairly convincingly. Kane is perhaps best known for both narrating and voicing Yoda on *Star Wars: The Clone Wars*.

In a nod to *Halloween II*, The Chordettes' *Mr. Sandman* can be heard twice in this film, once at the beginning and again in Keri Tate's SUV.

John Ottman was brought onto the film, replacing Alan Howarth as the resident composer, to bring a "Hitchcockian" vibe to the film.

Dimension Films were unhappy with composer John Ottman's original score and brought in Marco Beltrami to re-score the film using music from other movies.

Tom Kane is credited as "Voice Over" in the end credits scroll rather than "Dr. Loomis."

Chris Durand is simply credited as "Michael."

Halloween H20 was edited by Patrick Lussier, who also cut together the first three *Scream* movies. He went on to direct the *My Bloody Valentine* remake, *Drive Angry* and *Prophecy 3: The Ascent*.

HALLOWEEN H20

A handful of cuts to language and violence are made for the film's television version. Additionally, Jimmy doesn't steal any beer while investigating Marion's house.

This film stands as the shortest *Halloween* entry in the entire franchise at 86 minutes.

Dimension Films told the *LA Times* that an additional $15 million was spent marketing the film beyond the budget.

Halloween's seventh was originally supposed to open in October like most of its predecessors had, but was bumped up by the studio to August.

Halloween H20 opened in third place at the box office, bested by the also new *Snake Eyes* and unable to unseat *Saving Private Ryan* from the top spot. Despite the lower debut, it grossed $16.1 million opening weekend. It dropped to sixth place the following weekend before disappearing from the top ten.

The final musical cue was neither by John Ottman nor Marco Beltrami, but a direct port of John Carpenter's theme.

The film grossed $55 million at the domestic box office.

The cast of *Mystery Science Theater 3000* jokingly referred to this film as "*Halloween: Water*" in *their 2nd Annual Summer Blockbuster Review* special in which they riffed on the film's trailer.

Jamie Lee Curtis and Michelle Williams participated in a special "Scream Queen" photo shoot for the cover of *Entertainment Weekly* to promote this film.

To promote the film, Dimension Films unveiled a "*Halloween H20* Clip of the Day" every day across the week leading up to the film's release date.

This sequel features a portion of the song *What's This Life For?* by the band Creed. The band incorporated clips from the film in their music video for the song.

This film marked the first time any *Halloween* series cast member (Jamie Lee Curtis) went on *Live with Regis and Kathy Lee* to promote a *Halloween* sequel.

On Saturday, July 11, 1998, the cast of *Halloween H20*

HALLOWEEN H20

gathered at Planet Hollywood in Beverly Hills to present a prop from the film into their collection. Jamie Lee Curtis, Josh Hartnett, Michelle Williams and Adam Arkin along with Kevin Williams and Moustapha Akkad were on hand for the event. The prop? The red fire axe used to decapitate Michael Myers.

The film's Westwood premiere boasted a lengthy celebrity guest list that included Seth Green, Christina Ricci, John Ritter, Jessica Biel and Jamie Lee Curtis' father, Tony. Cast members in attendance for the event included Jamie Lee Curtis, Josh Hartnett, Michelle Williams, Joseph Gordon-Levitt, Janet Leigh, LL Cool J, Adam Arkin and Jodi Lyn O'Keefe.

When this film debuted onto DVD, it did so with a case that advertised an audio commentary by Steve Miner and Jamie Lee Curtis that was never actually recorded. The goof was caught only upon release and subsequent issues of the film omitted mention of the missing supplement.

HALLOWEEN RESURRECTION

Directed by Rick Rosenthal

Written by Larry Brand & Sean Hood
Story by Larry Brand

Jamie Lee Curtis (Laurie Strode)
Busta Rhymes (Freddie Harris)
Bianca Kajlich (Saya Moyer)
Katee Sackhoff (Jen)
Sean Patrick Thomas (Rudy)
Daisy McCrackin (Donna)
Thomas Ian Nichols (Bill)
Tyra Banks (Nora)

HALLOWEEN RESURRECTION

Originally titled *Hall8ween* and *Halloween: The Homecoming*, the producers instead wanted a title that assured audiences Michael Myers would return.

Halloween II's Rick Rosenthal returned to direct this film, making him the only director to helm two films in the franchise up until that point.

The filmmakers briefly considered having Laurie Strode commit suicide out of guilt for beheading an innocent man in the previous film, but decided against it.

Part of the genesis of this film was to acknowledge the franchise's massive online following.

Screenwriter Larry Brand created the film's story as a reverse-take on Orson Welles' 1938 *War of the Worlds* radio broadcast, which is actually one of the most novel ideas in the entire project. Whereas that broadcast was about the public believing something fictional was real (an alien invasion dramatized by Welles himself), *Halloween 8* was to be about the public believing something real was fictional (Michael actually killing the web contestants).

Halloween 6's Daniel Farrands wrote an unused script for this film.

Larry Brand's first job in the motion picture industry was as production assistant to Orson Welles. He named the Nurse Wells character in this film's opening after her.

(It is a hell of a lot shorter walk than I could have imagined from one of the greatest filmmakers of all time to *this* particular film.)

While Larry Brand is credited with the film's story, the shooting script was written by Brand and Sean Hood. I would love to tell you right now that the earliest versions of this screenplay actually held promise and did not contain Freddie Harris kung-fu'ing Michael Myers, but… "trick or treat, motherfucker."

The paramedic-switch-out twist that allowed the series to continue in this film was actually leaked to the internet mere days after *Halloween H20* hit theaters. It was practically lost, however, in a sea of other rumors and largely disregarded.

Rick Rosenthal originally pitched to Moustapha Akkad that they film four different endings and randomly place them in

HALLOWEEN RESURRECTION

theaters across the country, not informing audiences which ending they would be treated to. Akkad shot this idea down.

In the original script, Dangertainment was going to be called Netertainment.

An earlier version of Harold's dialogue after Michael hands him the bloody knife contained brief mention of Michael and Dr. Loomis being burned in the Haddonfield Memorial fire. Excising this was likely wise as reminding fans of the new sequel-erasing timeline as well as magically-disappearing-burn-scars continuity goof would have gained the filmmakers no points.

This film marks the first Myers-centric *Halloween* without appearance or mention of Dr. Loomis.

Harold seriously messes up the body counts of all three *Halloween* films he details (*Halloween*, *Halloween II* and *Halloween H20*). There is simply no way Michael's official count according to media outlets and law enforcement matches what he says, even ignoring the *Return/Revenge/Curse* trilogy.

This film seems to not mind that its predecessor also had characters name Sara and Charley in major roles.

The name of Jennifer Danzig's character is a nod to Misfits band member Glenn Danzig. The Misfits have songs titled *Halloween* and *Halloween II*, the latter of which would wind up in Rob Zombie's *Halloween*.

If there is one positive thing about this script, it is that it offers a reasonable explanation as to where Michael Myers has been quietly hiding the past two decades – his own home. And while someone would likely have found him hiding upstairs, *Resurrection* reveals that he has an underground hideout.

Halloween 4's Dwight Little turned down the opportunity to direct this film.

Only one cast member returns from the previous *Halloween*: Jamie Lee Curtis.

Jamie Lee Curtis was contractually obligated to make a small cameo at the beginning of this film, but chose to expand the screen time of her appearance in order to properly send off the character of Laurie Strode.

HALLOWEEN RESURRECTION

Sean Patrick Thomas receives a "Special Appearance By" nod in the opening credits. Forgive me, but what was so special about his appearance?

Jacinda Barrett was originally cast as Sara Moyer but dropped out of the film due to a scheduling conflict.

Although Bianca Kajlich was originally cast as Jennifer Danzig, she was moved into the role of Sara in the wake of Jacinda Barrett's departure.

The filmmakers briefly considered casting Danielle Harris as a role in the film.

Brad Loree was the first actor considered for the role of Michael in this film.

Brad Loree's first task after being hired was to fly to Los Angeles to have a cast made of his head so that the film's masks could be custom-fitted to his head.

This was the first film and only film in the series to film in Canada.

After Bianca Kajlich switched parts, the role of Jennifer Danzig was unfilled. The filmmakers moved Katee Sackhoff into the part, whom they had originally cast as Donna Chang.

Kyle Labine appears both in this film and *Freddy vs Jason*, meaning he figures into the final original timeline films of Michael Myers, Freddy Krueger and Jason Voorhees before they were turned into remakes.

The filmmakers then filled the newly vacated part of Donna Chang with Daisy McCrackin.

Bianca Kajlich had not seen any of the *Halloween* films prior to being cast in this sequel. To her credit, she did immediately go out and watch them all.

This was also the first and only film in the series to use a specially built set for the *exterior* of the Myers House.

The newly filmed flashback material from *Halloween H20*'s conclusion was not captured at the same location from that film, but rather a close approximation of it. Those with an eye for detail can spot the differences.

HALLOWEEN RESURRECTION

Principal photography began on May 14, 2001.

Once on set, the filmmakers realized exactly to what extent Bianca Kajlich could not scream – which was hardly at all. As a result, she was dubbed by a professional voice actress in post-production.

Director Rick Rosenthal makes a cameo early on in the film as Dr. Mixter, the name of a character from *Halloween II*, which he also directed.

As on *Halloween II*, Jamie Lee Curtis is again wearing a wig to simulate having longer hair.

The scene in which the contestants and press arrive at the Myers House was partly shot in an actual neighborhood and partly on set. It switches seamlessly between the two locations. (So when Busta is staring at the Myers House, he is actually staring at a random home instead.)

The warehouse roof of the studio can be seen in several Myers House shots, particularly when Michael is kicked out of the window and hung on computer cables.

Michael Myers descending from the pipes in this film is a nod to the same maneuver in *Halloween H20*.

Bianca Kajlich presented Jamie Lee Curtis with a decorative crown as a gift to acknowledge her scream queen status.

Jamie Lee Curtis in turn gave Bianca Kajlich a bottle of Vick's Throat Spray for all of the screaming that would soon be expected of her on the film.

Although Tyra Banks' Nora can be seen consuming alcohol in the film, Banks herself does not drink.

Michael Myers speaks (or rather groans) in this film after more than thirty years of remaining silent while being punched, run over, stabbed and shot multiple times. Yes, it is finally in *Halloween Resurrection* that Michael groans in pain after Busta Ryhme's Freddie Harris electrocutes Michael in the nuts.

Michael Myers gets goddamn electrocuted in his goddamn nuts in this film. Can we all agree now and forever that this sequel is an abomination beyond measure?

Total Body Count: 10

HALLOWEEN RESURRECTION

A framed picture of Josh Hartnett's John Tate can be seen in Laurie's room at the hospital.

An earlier version of the shooting script included a line that revealed John eventually just stopped visiting his mother at the sanitarium as catatonia set in.

Special Makeup Effects Creator Gary J. Tunnicliffe cameos as a police officer in the film.

Although this film begins with opening credits, the title is not shown until just past the sixteen-minute mark.

This film was subject to studio-ordered reshoots that took place across September and October, 2001.

Rumors about trouble with Rick Rosenthal began to circulate during *Halloween Resurrection*'s post-production so strongly that Moustapha Akkad had to issue a public statement declaring that Rosenthal was still at the helm and that the film was okay.

Katee Sackhoff's name is mis-spelled in the opening credits as "Katee Sachoff." It appears correctly in the end credit scroll, however.

The original release date for this film was September 21, 2001. Studio-ordered reshoots pushed the release back to July 12, 2002. When you think about it, this was probably for the best as ten days after the 9/11 attacks might not have been an ideal time to drop a slasher film.

When the film was finally released, it landed in fourth place at the box office behind *Men in Black II*, *Road to Perdition* and *Reign of Fire* to capture $12.2 million. It would slip to eighth place the following weekend before dropping out of the top ten films.

This sequel opened on 1,954 theater screens.

The box office take for *Halloween*'s eighth was $30.3 million.

This film's long-awaited trailer finally debuted in theaters before prints of *Jason X*.

Ever the trendsetter, Michael Myers apparently set the stage for Freddy Krueger and Jason Voorhees to go Canadian

HALLOWEEN RESURRECTION

several years later in *Freddy vs Jason*, the first of either franchise to shoot out of the United States. Chucky the Killer Doll, however, fled to Romania instead for *Seed of Chucky*.

The studio opted to re-use Jamie Lee Curtis' likeness from *Halloween H20*'s marketing materials on this sequel's poster. As a result, Laurie Strode appears with short hair on the poster instead of with longer, messier hair as in the film.

Rick Rosenthal was hopeful that the DVD edition of the film would allow viewers to switch seamlessly between the different character's video feeds. This idea was not realized.

In addition to playing Michael Myers, Brad Loree also tested for the role of Jason Voorhees in *Freddy vs Jason*.

Brad Loree was hopeful that he might return to play Michael again in *Halloween 9* and volunteered himself for the role before the series was rebooted.

Several years after filming, Brad Loree became roommates with Brad Sihvon, the actor that played Charley. So basically, Michael Myers became roomies with the tripod-kill victim.

Sean Hood was none too pleased with how the film turned out and has since publicly stated he would prefer his name no longer be associated with the film.

Believe it or not, the idea for *Halloween Resurrection* was actually stolen and bastardized in Adam Matalon's 2008 cinematic suppository *Death on Demand* in which a web broadcast contest is held in the abandoned home of a serial killer to see who can stay the entire night… only for the killer to actually show up. Oh and the serial killer offed his entire family two decades earlier on *Thanksgiving*. Who is Adam Matalon, you ask? Well, his most-respectable credit appears to be as stage manager on *Elmo's Potty Time*. (I swear I'm not making this up.)

HALLOWEEN RESURRECTION

Rob Zombie's
HALLOWEEN

Directed by Rob Zombie

Written by Rob Zombie

Scout Taylor-Compton (Laurie Strode)
Malcolm McDowell (Dr. Sam Loomis)
Sheri Moon Zombie (Deborah Myers)
Danielle Harris (Annie Brackett)
Kristina Klebe (Lynda van der Klok)
Hannah Hall (Judith Myers)
Daeg Farech (Young Michael Myers)
Brad Dourif (Sheriff Lee Brackett)
Danny Trejo (Ismael Cruz)
Tyler Mane (Michael Myers)

RZ's HALLOWEEN

The tragic death of Moustapha Akkad greatly delayed this film's development, which for a time was going to continue the original series timeline rather than remake it.

This film very nearly became a Michael vs Pinhead movie, dubbed by fans as *Helloween*.

Rob Zombie appeared in the *Halloween: 25 Years of Terror* documentary prior to being announced as the remake's director.

Rob Zombie consulted John Carpenter out of professional respect prior to officially signing onto the production. John Carpenter's only advise to Rob Zombie was: "Make it your own."

Rob Zombie and John Carpenter were actually friends and colleagues having worked together years earlier when Zombie contributed a song to Carpenter's *Escape from L.A.* soundtrack.

The film was given a $15 million budget.

An early draft of the screenplay leaked online prior to the film's release. It contained a number of discarded concepts, many controversial to *Halloween* purists.

Although this film has been branded a remake, a considerable portion of it is spent exploring a time glossed over in the original *Halloween*. Although oft-talked about by Dr. Loomis, audiences have never before seen any of Michael's time inside Smith's Grove Warren-County Sanitarium.

At one point, Rob Zombie unsuccessfully pitched that he be allowed to make two *Halloween* movies simultaneously, one leading up to Michael's escape from Smith's Grove Warren-County Sanitarium and another on Halloween night.

Big Joe Grizzlys line about having "failure to communicate" is a nod to Strothers Martin in *Cool Hand Luke*.

When we last found Dr. Loomis at the start of *Halloween: The Curse of Michael Myers*, he was just beginning to write a book. In this film, Dr. Loomis finishes and publishes a book on his time working with Michael Myers.

Annie Brackett is the only character to die in the original *Halloween* but survive the remake.

RZ's HALLOWEEN

Deborah Myers is the only character in the entire script to die and not be killed by Michael Myers. She is also the only suicide in the entire ten-film (as of now) *Halloween* franchise.

Total Body Count: 17 (with one of those being suicide)

Emma Stone auditioned for the role of Laurie Strode.

Skyler Gsondo originally auditioned for the part of young Michael Myers but was cast as Tommy Doyle instead.

Danielle Harris makes her triumphant return to the *Halloween* franchise after having bowed out of *Halloween: The Curse of Michael Myers*. She was proactive in lobbying for a part in the film.

If Danny Trejo's advice to young Michael to "look beyond the walls" of the prison seem unusually sincere, it could be because Trejo spent time behind bars himself and has since worked closely with at-risk youth to guide them away from a life of crime.

Rob Zombie has candidly admitted that he did not initially want to cast Danielle Harris in the film, citing her prior work on the franchise as a hindrance. She remains the only cast member to return from any of the preceding eight films.

It would not be a *Halloween* set without some measure of romance – Sherri Moon-Zombie is (to no one's surprise reading this) the wife of Rob Zombie.

Malcolm McDowell deliberately chose not to watch any of the preceding films so as not to be influenced by Donald Pleasance's take on Dr. Loomis.

Although not exactly the closest of colleagues, Malcolm McDowell and Donald Pleasance had become friends years earlier after McDowell took Pleasance out for drinks following one of the latter's theater performances.

The entire main cast of *The Devil's Rejects* appears in this film: Sherri Moon-Zombie, Bill Moseley, Sid Haig and Leslie Easterbrook.

Brad Douriff, Malcolm McDowell and Clint Howard have all made appearances in *Star Trek* productions.

RZ's HALLOWEEN

At twenty-nine, Danielle Harris was eleven years older than the character she played.

Tyler Mane stands far and above his predecessors as the tallest performer to play Michael Myers yet. He clocks in at a whopping 6'9.

Tyler Mane, who had previously sported long locks, had gotten a short haircut one week prior to receiving Rob Zombie's call to appear in the film as Michael Myers. As such, Mane was forced to endure a troublesome wig throughout filming.

When Danielle Harris first received the script, she simply assumed and had accepted the likely fact that Annie Brackett was going to die in the remake just as in the original. She was ecstatic to read that her character did, in fact, survive the bloodbath.

Tyler Mane closely studied the preceding *Halloween* films, minus part three, against the advice of Rob Zombie who did not want him to be influenced by what had come before.

Mane reportedly became a genuine *Halloween* fan after viewing the entire series.

Brad Douriff had not seen any *Halloween* movies prior to filming and sought to keep it that way. He vowed, possibly jokingly, in press for the film that he would never watch it again after the premiere, owing to the fact that he simply does not enjoy horror films.

Max Van Ville originally auditioned for the part of Steve, but was cast as Paul instead.

Rob Zombie wanted to cast genre performers in roles opposite their stereotype. Brad Douriff plays a trustworthy sheriff, Clint Howard is an ordinary hospital administrator, Danny Trejo appears as a sweet, consoling orderly and Lew Temple plays a disgusting redneck.

William Forsyth had actually broken his leg shortly before filming and the cast he sports in the film was quite real. Rob Zombie had originally only scripted for Ronnie to have a broken arm.

This film returned to Pasadena, CA to film – the first series entry to shoot here since *Halloween II*.

RZ's HALLOWEEN

Rob Zombie wanted to evoke the same look at the neighborhood in the original film and opted to film near many of the original *Halloween*'s locations. In some cases, Zombie literally shot across the street from them.

The Strode house from the original *Halloween* can be seen behind Michael when Laurie first sees him watching her from the library.

The bag from which Steve pulls the white mask from reads "Nichols Hardware," a subtle nod to the location in *Halloween* that Michael broke into and stole a mask, several knives and some rope.

Although Scout Taylor-Compton, Danielle Harris and Kristina Klebe were all playing characters in high school, only Compton was actually a teenager at the time. This mirrored Jamie Lee's age and position relative to her co-stars on the original *Halloween*.

When Laurie calls 911, she mentions the house being on Winchester Road. The company that made the original *The Thing From Another World* was named Winchester.

White Zombie can be seen playing on television in the film. This was the film Rob Zombie titled his band of the same name after.

Rob Zombie makes a small cameo in the film as the police dispatcher who alerts Sheriff Brackett to the situation at the Wallace residence.

When young Michael Myers is first introduced, he is wearing a KISS shirt. Simultaneously, the "God of Thunder" by KISS can be heard on the soundtrack.

A portion of the Truck Wash scene was filmed on February 29th, 2007, which happened to be Ken Foree's fifty-ninth birthday. The crew treated him to a birthday cake on set.

Rob Zombie gave regular production updates and debuted photos from filming on his official MySpace account.

MySpace, for you younger readers, was the social media predecessor to Facebook. Go ask your Grandparents – they'll tell you all about it.

The Thing From Another World plays on television Halloween night in both this film and John Carpenter's original.

RZ's HALLOWEEN

Tommy's Halloween costume is that of The Misfits iconic mascot "The Crimson Ghost." Rob Zombie is an enormous Misfits fan and includes the band on the remake's soundtrack.

The line about Michael having strangely become Dr. Loomis' best friend was not in the shooting script and ad-libbed by Malcolm McDowell.

Several shots of Danielle Harris' encounter with Michael Myers were filmed twice – once topless for the film and a second time clothed for use in advertising.

The Monkee's drummer Mickey Dolenz cameos as the salesman Dr. Loomis buys a gun from.

At one point in the film, Ronnie says that Michael would wind up cutting off his manhood and changing his name to "Michelle." Daeg Farech's next role was in *Hancock* as a trash-talking French kid named Michel (spoke "Michelle.")

Daeg Farech was allowed to keep young Michael's clown costume.

Tyler Mane insisted upon playing adult Michael in every scene of the film including stunts, the one exception being when Michael and Laurie crash through the upstairs window of the Myers house. For this one shot, stuntman Casey Hendershot took Mane's place.

The task of recreating Michael Myer's iconic mask went to effects-master Wayne Toth.

He had one week to sculpt the new mask using only reference photos from the original film.

Because the mask was mold-fitted to Tyler Mane's head, he was unable to wear his wig underneath the mask.

The mask breathing you hear in the film is actually Tyler Mane. The performer was required to step into the ADR booth wearing several different masks in post-production and breathe in various ways.

Rob Zombie had originally planned for Deborah Myer's stripping to be set to Alice Cooper's "Only Women Bleed" and the scene was filmed while the song played. It was only in post-production that Zombie changed his mind and the song to Nazareth's "Love Hurts."

RZ's HALLOWEEN

An unfinished workprint of the remake was released prior to the film's theatrical release featuring different editing, alternate/deleted scenes and a temporary music track.

Adrienne Barbeau's part was cut from the film entirely.

The studio was hesitant to release the film near Halloween due to the wildly popular Saw franchise having already claimed that release date with Saw IV. (The taglines read, "If it's Halloween, it must be Saw.")

This film's trailer debuted with the Quentin Tarrantinto/Robert Rodriquez double-feature *Grindhouse*.

At 109 minutes, this is the longest *Halloween* movie up until this point.

Contrary to some reports, several cast members were contracted to appear in a sequel should one have ever been made.

Rob Zombie's *Halloween* earned the franchise its first Razzie nomination for Worst Film of the Year. It did not win.

Given that he had only just turned eleven, Daeg Farech was allowed to watch his scenes early in the film at the premiere screening but then required to leave for the more violent second and third acts.

In a bizarre twist, the first trailer to Rob Zombie's very-real *Halloween* remake debuted alongside the fake trailer for the made-up film *Werewolf Women of the SS*, which also played before *Grindhouse*.

Anticipating questions from fans about it, original Shape Nick Castle first saw the film on his iPad during a flight to New Jersey's Monster Mania 17 convention. He later admitted that it was neither the best way nor place in which to view a *Halloween* film. While he was respectful in his comments about it, he confessed that he was not a fan of Rob Zombie's approach.

Original young Michael Myers Will Sandin felt much the same, lamenting the lack of mystery in the new film while still hailing it as a "really good remake" at Monster Mania 13.

At the same event, the original face of Michael, Tony Moran, made no effort to sugarcoat his opinion of the

RZ's HALLOWEEN

remake: "I love Rob Zombie and his music and a couple of his movies. But… you paint a picture and that's that. Then somebody tries to recreate your picture, tries to repaint your picture and you're like *'Are you out of your fuckin' mind?'* Now granted, I'm not scoring any points with Rob Zombie here, but he's got nothing on me so I don't give a shit."

HALLOWEEN II

Directed by Rob Zombie

Written by Rob Zombie

Scout Taylor-Compton (Laurie Strode)
Malcolm McDowell (Dr. Sam Loomis)
Danielle Harris (Annie Brackett)
Brad Douriff (Sheriff Lee Brackett)
Brea Grant (Mya Rockwell)
Mary Birdsong (Nancy McDonald)
Sheri Moon Zombie (Deborah Myers)
Chase Wright Vanek (Young Michael Myers)
Tyler Mane (Michael Myers)

HALLOWEEN II

Rob Zombie strongly rejected the notion of returning for a sequel while promoting the first film.

The film was originally to be directed by the French filmmaking duo responsible for *High Tension*, Julien Maury and Alexandre Bustillo. They parted ways with the production over creative differences shortly before Rob Zombie re-enlisted.

On December 15, 2008, *Variety* announced that Rob Zombie was officially in talks to both write and direct the next film in the franchise.

Rob Zombie is only the second director to helm two films in the *Halloween* series and the only director two helm two consecutive entries.

This is the first *Halloween* film in which adult Michael Myers speaks. His only word? "Die!"

Like its predecessor, this film was given a $15 million budget.

In the theatrical version of the film, one year has passed since Michael "came home." In the director's cut, two years have passed.

This is also the first *Halloween* in which an unmasked adult Michael freely walks about.

Dr. Loomis' line at the press conference for his book, "Let's get things nice and clear," is a nod to a similar line he spoke in *A Clockwork Orange*

This film has two parallels with the original *Halloween II*. It begins with Laurie Strode being transferred to Haddonfield Memorial Hospital and being followed by Michael. Both films also feature a brief return to the Myers House where a news crew is taping outside.

The scene in which a young boy asks Michael if he is a giant is an homage to a similar scene in *Son of Frankenstein*.

Total Body Count: 19

In early February, Rob Zombie announced through his official website that Scout Taylor-Compton, Malcolm McDowell and Tyler Mane would all return for the sequel.

HALLOWEEN II

Tyler Mane was given plenty of advance notice on this film to begin letting his hair grow out. Consequently, he did not need a wig this time around for the role of Michael Myers.

This is the first Rob Zombie film not to star Bill Moseley, Sid Haig or Tom Towles.

Bill Moseley was originally cast as Uncle Seymour Coffins and underwent makeup tests for the role. Rob Zombie even released an image from these tests online to announce the casting. Moseley was forced to drop out of the role, however, due to scheduling conflicts.

This film has several returning performers from Rob Zombie's *Halloween*. They include Scout Taylor-Compton, Malcolm McDowell, Tyler Mane, Danielle Harris, Brad Douriff, Sherri Moon-Zombie and Daniel Roebuck.

There was serious concern early on that Daeg Farech may have aged too much to play young Michael again. There was hope that by using oversized props and furniture he might appear smaller and younger. Camera tests executed using this technique did not yield the desired results.

A brief glimpse of Daeg Farech's camera test can be seen in the film's first trailer. Rob Zombie objected to these being included, insisting they were never meant to be in the film or its marketing campaign.

After Bill Moseley's departure, the part of Uncle Seymour Coffins was played by Jeff Daniel Phillips, who also played Howard Boggs in the film. This makes Phillips the second performer to have dual-roles in a *Halloween* film, the first being Dick Warlock in the original *Halloween II*.

Jeff Daniel Phillips may be more familiar to moviegoers as the caveman that appeared in GEICO commercials for several years.

Tyler Mane is only the second performer to play Michael Myers twice and the only performer to do so in two consecutive films.

Brea Grant was thirty-two-years-old performing as a nineteen-year-old character.

Chris Hardwick, better known to *Walking Dead* fans as the charismatic host of *Talking Dead*, appears briefly in this film as a talk show host interviewing Dr. Loomis.

HALLOWEEN II

Rob Zombie originally wanted Bob Saget as Dr. Loomis' fellow guest on the talk show program. It was Chris Hardwick who suggested Weird Al, who then enthusiastically jumped the next flight to Georgia for a chance to play himself in a *Halloween* movie.

Despite this being her fourth appearance in a *Halloween* film, this was Danielle Harris' first time dying in the series.

Nurse Octavia Daniels was named for the performer that played her – Octavia Spencer.

This film features Caroline Williams in a small role as a doctor near the beginning of the film. Had Bill Moseley remained on the cast, it would have been their first film together since *Texas Chainsaw Massacre Part 2*, which was an enormous influence for Rob Zombie on *House of 1,000 Corpses*.

Neither Scout Taylor-Compton nor Danielle Harris have ever met Jamie Lee Curtis, though both have expressed a desire to do so someday.

The production moved to Georgia in order to take advantage of that state's lucrative tax benefits for movie shoots. It would become the first film in the series not to shoot on the West Coast.

Although the filmmakers were able to find a convincing double for the Californian Myers House, the structure still required substantial set dressing from the art department, including a more pronounced second floor balcony.

This film shot in an actual strip club for the Rabbit in Red scenes. Consequently, the eye holes on Chase Wright Vanek's clown mask were taped over for his time inside the club.

Although never explicitly stated in the film, Laurie and her friends are dressed as characters from *The Rocky Horror Picture Show*.

The flashback to Annie Brackett's childhood was chosen by the filmmakers from a handful of old home videocassette tapes that Danielle Harris' mother mailed to the production.

Michael's rotted, half-mask look was originally envisioned as being like the mask worn by the Phantom of the Opera.

HALLOWEEN II

Uncle Seymour Coffin's makeup and costume were directly lifted from the Vincent Price film *Madhouse*.

Malcolm McDowell wrapped his time on the film in eight days.

The original *Night of the Living Dead* can be seen playing on television in this film. It was also playing on television in the original *Halloween II*.

So can *Forbidden Planet* and *The Thing From Another World*, both of which were seen playing on television in the original *Halloween*.

Tyler Mane's favorite way to unwind after a long day on set was reportedly to retire to his trailer for a cigar and a glass of wine.

Michael's disheveled look in this film earned him the online nickname "Hobo Myers."

The iconic *Halloween* theme is not heard until the final shot of the film.

Tyler Mane returned again to record ADR for his role. Unlike in the previous film, Michael can actually be heard grunting in this film during several intense kills.

Captain Clegg and the Night Creatures, a fictional band that exists within the universe of the sequel, were given a full album release to coincide with the film's release. They also featured into several music videos that appeared online and on the film's home video release.

Rob Zombie was not fond of the trailers that were created to market the film, feeling they depicted it as a brainless slasher sequel.

An unused alternate trailer eventually leaked onto the internet, giving fans a very different look at the movie. It made excellent use of "Nights in White Satin" by The Moody Blues and featured more dialogue. Rob Zombie eventually commented that he much preferred the leaked trailer for better representing the film he made.

This film was released on August 28, 2009.

It debuted on 3,025 theater screens.

HALLOWEEN II

Halloween II was re-released to theaters on October 30, 2009 to capitalize on the holiday. It played on 1,083 screens and was unable to dethrone the latest *Saw* sequel.

This became the first film since *Halloween 5* not to suffer a workprint leak either before or after its theatrical release.

This film sold more than 200,000 home video units in its first week.

The poster for this film appears on the wall of a film theory classroom in *Scream 4*.

PURELY & SIMPLY EVIL

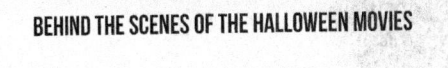

BEHIND THE SCENES OF THE HALLOWEEN MOVIES

PURELY & SIMPLY EVIL

PURELY & SIMPLY EVIL

Copyright 2013 New Arcata Books

This book is not approved by or related to the makers of the *Halloween* series.

BEHIND THE SCENES OF THE HALLOWEEN MOVIES